LIVING ABOARD

PROJECTS FOR MAKING A GOOD LIFE BETTER

By

Donald L. Boone

You will read words of wisdom that tell you, "Go as soon as you can." Most often they mean you should go cruising around the world as soon as you can, but, in a sense, this is mis-leading. You do not need to travel long distances to be cruising.

INTRODUCTION

As Lyn and I moved aboard each of our boats over the years, we soon found what changes were needed to accommodate our life styles aboard. To make them easier, and more comfortable for our cruising and living habits. I'd like to pass some of those on to you.

No one questions the ability of boating manufacturers to build boats, but when building them on a large scale production, they cannot please every potential owners' needs over the vessels life time. They construct a boat that is safe, reasonably easy to maintain, and as comfortable in most given boating conditions as possible. Of course, they build them as a sailing vessel, sailing, not as a live aboard facility. Especially the smaller boats, as larger boats have more room, thus more storage space and more area to lay about.

Boat length is controversial subject, I've met couples living on twenty-four footers who were quite happy, I've also met couples living on fifty footers who felt crowded. My largest boat, 'Star Gazer,' an Ackerman forty footer, was quite comfortable. At the same time our Cascade 29, 'Endless Summer', worked well for the two of us, though she was narrow of beam, yet sea kindly in heavy offshore storms. Our Catalina 30, 'Itchy Feet' carried us for many years, through heavy weather, and many ports of call.

Still, each boat required some sort of modification to suit our personal needs. It is my intention, in this book, to help you to make some decisions about what you may want to change aboard your boat. Perhaps some of our projects will work for you, or guide you, in considering how and why to make a few changes.

Many of the modifications we made to our boats were made while keeping an eye on the cruising funds we had available, and, with the items we felt would add to our creature comforts, also to make things easier while aboard. Not all of the projects in this book deal primarily with the creature comforts, while living aboard, some were made to improve the handling, or the maintenance of a boat. Perhaps some of our projects will work for you, or guide you in making a few changes.

TABLE OF CONTENTS

TOPSIDE
- Aft Storage lockers
- Anchor storage
- Baggy Wrinkles
- Bird nest on the foredeck
- Boom tents / Dodger
- Bow roller
- Bug screens
- Cure that dragging hatch cover
- Hatch boards, or Swinging doors
- Noises in the night
- Outboard motor storage
- Pushpit gates
- Simple showers

BELOW DECK
- Cook stoves
- Clothes storage
- Ice boxes
- Privacy curtains
- Refrigerators
- Storage areas

ELECTRICAL
- Auto-pilots
- Automatic anchor lights
- Television antenna

ENGINES
- Venting engine odors

BILGES
- Bilge alarms
- Holding tanks
- Using ice melt water

MAINTENANCE
- Careening
- Dinghy storage
- Getting high
- Simple moorings
- Strut bearings

NAVIGATION
- Home made speed logs
- Making your own charts
- Using celestial navigation anywhere

USEFUL INFORMATION
- Anchoring
- Animals aboard
- Children aboard
- Living aboard

TOPSIDE

ANCHOR STORAGE

If your boat does not have a bowsprit where an anchor can be permanently mounted, this may be a familiar scenario to you. It's late and you're entering your chosen anchorage for the night. You've made your choice as to where you want to put the hook down and the boat is now drifting with the engine at idle, the transmission in neutral. You go forward to drop the anchor, but first you have to lift the Jib, or Jib bag off the foredeck and fasten it up out of the way.

You think it's out of the way and you're ready, but you discover the bag is still covering the front corner of the lid to your anchor well. All of this just needs to get moved to get to the anchor. Next you lean down into the anchor well and lift out the heavy anchor and lay it on deck, then you pull the line and chain out on deck as well. You close the lid to the storage space, and again lift the anchor off the deck, manipulate it through your bow pulpit and finally drop it into the water so you can finish your anchoring procedure. Of course by now your boat has drifted away from the spot you wanted to anchor in, in the first place and you have to motor back to it again.

The problem is you've gone to all of this work just to get the anchor ready to put over the side, and it is not necessary simply because there is an easier way to do this. There are no doubt a great variety of anchor mounting devices on the market that you can choose from, but nothing quite as simple, or inexpensive, as the method I'm proposing.

Measure the size of your anchor stock and the chain as you hold them collapsed together in your hand. That is with the chain lying alongside the anchor stock where the anchor and chain come together with the shackle. Then purchase a piece of white PVC pipe large enough in diameter to allow your anchor, fastening shackle, and chain to slip down inside of the PVC pipe.

Your tool requirements for this project are quite small. You'll need a hacksaw for cutting the plastic pipe, a screwdriver for the large hose clamps you'll need to go around the PVC pipe, and that of your stainless steel pulpit tubing. Perhaps you will also need a small pair of wire cutters, or a pocket knife, for cutting off the ends of the wire ties.

Stainless steel hose clamps work best for fastening the PVC in place where it works best while you are pulling in your anchor and anchor rode. I found that using nylon wire ties kept the ends of the hose clamps down tight against the pipe so they would not snag on other things in the area, such as clothing or sailbags.

The cut length of the pipe would normally run from the deck to the top of your bow pulpit. A wood rasp works well in shaping the PVC so it will conform as needed. Also cut any odd angles the PVC tube may require to fit at the deck level, or inside the stanchion of the bow pulpit.

Once you have finished this simple storage device, and you're pulling your anchor up, you merely lift the anchor up, and drop the anchor shank, shackle and chain down inside the PVC tube.

One more item to consider: You can cut a notch in the anchor well lid to allow the spare chain and rode to slip below out of the way until needed.

I discovered an added bonus when I added this anchor storage device to my pulpit. The anchor line comes aboard up over my bow roller, then to a good solid deck cleat just beyond the PVC tubing. The four-inch PVC tube is large enough that the anchor rode rubs against it while lying to the anchor.

One night as we lay sleeping in the vee berth, with our plow anchor down, the wind picked up. I woke to the sound of the anchor rode rubbing against the PVC tube as the nylon anchor line stretched to hold the weight of the boat at the end of a swing. As the weight of the hull eased off, the line would again rub against the tube.

The sound was not annoying, and I found it comforting to listen to. Comforting, because I could tell when the boat finished swinging on the anchor and when the pressure was off the line. I knew we were snug and not dragging the hook, and in a sense it became an anchor lookout for me without my having to go topside to have a look at the conditions. I've never been concerned about the line chafing because of the large diameter of the PVC tube. When you are not traveling, you can put your anchor away if needed, but here's a drawing of how this method might look from above.

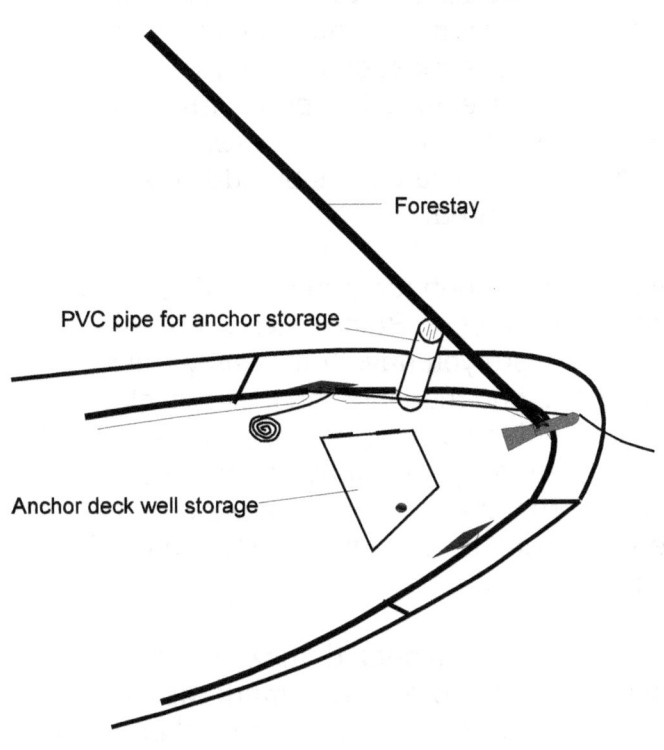

AFT STORAGE LOCKER

We've all been through the routine of trying to reach a can of paint or varnish, maybe a toolbox, whatever, and it's always at the bottom of that aft locker. You know the one built into the hull under the cockpit seat, the one that a small child can stand up in. The same one that when you try to reach deep down inside it bruises your ribs.

Well, there is a simple way of raising that stuff up to an acceptable height, and in fact you can place the stuff you use most on a higher level than the material you use less. The boat's manufacturer at least made a locker for you to use, you just have to make it usable. You do this by adding shelves into this locker aft area.

If you have enough room to get inside this locker, take everything out. Before you climb inside the locker, be sure you have the items you'll need to plan, mark, and measure the locker's interior. Such as a carpenter's collapsible tape measure, a good pencil, or marking pen, maybe some paper for notes. Perhaps a cushion to sit on, and plan on an area for your legs and knees. No, you won't be comfortable

Once you're in and settled, make a mark at the forward inboard corner. This mark will be the location down from the top of the locker where you want the shelf to be added, or up from the depth you require under the shelf. Then mark a horizontal line aft until it meets the end of the locker, or the bottom of the hull, whichever comes first. You can do this by measuring down from inside the top of the locker.

Do the same thing from the original mark in the corner, to the forward outside corner of the hull, or of the locker. These lines may not be level, just the same distance down from the top all of the way around. I suggest the use of a black marking pen because this ink is water proof and will not easily rub off before you're finished. Now you're ready to begin your construction.

Don't skimp on the wood strips you're going to use to support your shelf, because in the long run you may have quite a bit of weight sitting on the shelf.

I purchased a standard 2.0" X 4.0", then cut it in half length wise, this provided me with two 2.0" X 2.0"s. In some lumber suppliers you can purchase these in precut dimensions.

Okay, measure the length of your longest piece required, and plan on having to possibly taper the end to fit against the hull. If it requires tapering, be sure to cut the piece a little longer to compensate for the loss of wood as it is tapered. A decision has to be made as to how you are going to fasten these shelf supports. You can use fiberglass and resin, or you can simply use stainless steel screws.

I pre-drilled the holes in my wood supports and marked the mounting areas through the holes. Using this method allows you to drill carefully through any bulkhead, and then you can use a tap for the size of thread of the screws you are going to use unless you plan on using nuts on the other side. In my case I used 1/4-20 tap. You just want to be careful of what is on the other side, if you don't already know.

Once you have the wooden shelf supports in place the tough part starts. I suggest you use at least 1/2" plywood anything less may lack the strength needed.

You should make your shelf a two piece arrangement, this will allow you to remove one half without having to take everything out of the locker to get underneath for the other stuff.

Start with the inner half, normally the largest, and cut it to fit the entire length of the locker. You may be able to cut one piece off the outside aft corner by making a rough judgement, then you'll have to put the piece down in the locker to see where it doesn't fit, then cut a little more off. Do this until you have both halves finished and fitted to the contours of the hull where it is required.

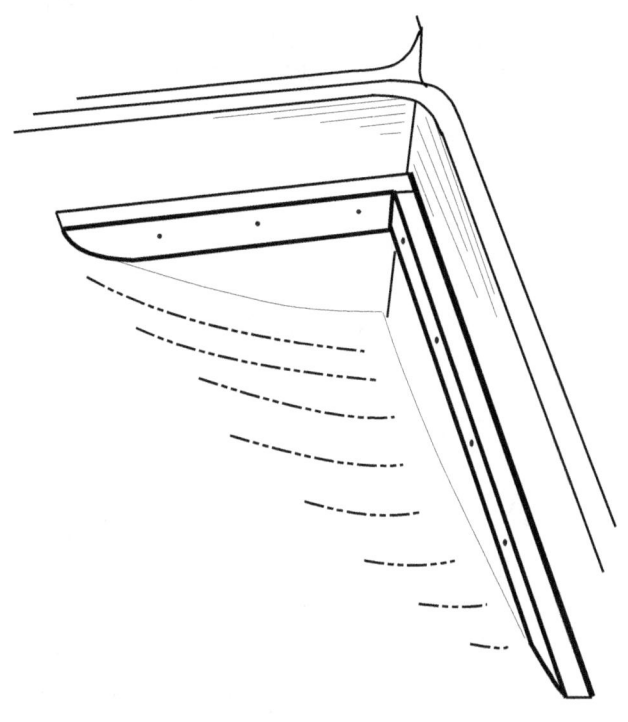

You might want to consider putting finger holes in each piece so you can lift them out easily. You may have more time than money involved in this project, but when you go to the lumber yard, ask if they have some scrap pieces of plywood around. Often these can be had for a very reasonable price.

Once you have this finished, you can store items that need to be kept cool, in the bottom section. Should you need even more storage area, and if your locker is deep enough, you could add a second shelf above the lower one.

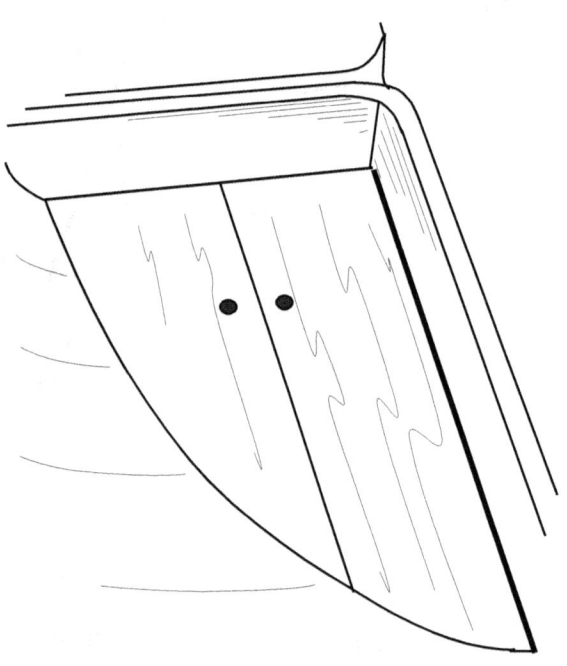

BIRDNESTS ON THE FOREDECK

Nearly all of us have done this, looked down at your feet while standing on the foredeck, only to see a pile of tangled anchor line. It seems as if all you did was take it out of the locker and put it down---the knotted mess came out of nowhere. Now, however, it has to be straightened out before the anchor goes over the side.

It was on one of these occasions, as my wife helped me sort the mess out, that she said, "Why don't you just chain stitch it?"

My reply was simply, "Do what?"

"Chain stitch the anchor line before you put it away in the anchor well."

I didn't have a clue what she was talking about, but while we were anchored here for a few days I got out my book on 'Sailing Knots,' by Geoffrey Budsworth, and on page 125 I found a drawing of how to make a chain stitch. If I hadn't had that book I could have asked Lyn, but you know, this is a guy thing.

It's actually quite simple to do. You start by making three or four loops of your anchor line. Start with the end in your hand and go down around your elbow and back to your hand. This will leave loops of about two feet in diameter in your line.

When you first start this process, the whole thing will seem to be too loose; not to worry it will tighten up as you progress.

Start by laying the coiled loops on your foredeck and then pull a small loop of line, from the end you've coiled, up and inside the coil. This is the line that goes out to the anchor, not the loose end you are working with.

Leave about a six-inch loop of slack above the height of the coil, then holding the first loop with one hand, pull a second loop up on the outside of the coil of line. Holding the first loop with one hand, pass the second loop up through the loop from the inside. You should now have a loop through a loop.

Repeat the process by holding your new loop with one hand while you pull more line back under the coiled line on deck to form a new loop on the inside. Which of course goes up through the loop from the outside, and so it goes for as much line as you want to store in this manner. When you're finished, you will have a ring of coiled line, but most of it will be fashioned out of an ongoing chain of loops, each one through the one before.

To finish, you make your last loop long enough to make a loose overhand knot around the line going to your anchor chain. There, you see, it does look like a bird's nest.

There is more than one benefit to using this method of anchor line storage. First, it keeps your anchor line from fouling when it's placed in your anchor well. Second, when you have it topside and stowed on your foredeck, it will be a neat tidy package while the anchor is holding you in place.

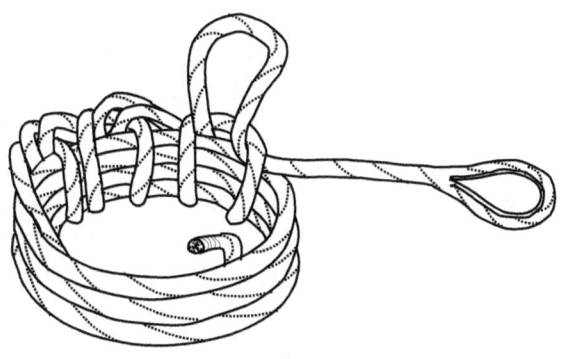

BOOM TENT, or DODGER

Dodgers can be a spendy item for any boat, but on a sailboat a boom tent may not be. My preference for traveling is the dodger to keep the weather out of the main cabin, and to provide a wind break for the soul who is topside. At anchorage, or at the docks, I prefer a boom tent.

A full length boom tent will shade your entire cockpit, thus providing plenty of room for your afternoon nap in the shade when needed, or for the comfort of guests that drop by. I've spent many a summer in the cockpit under a boom tent reading or writing. Of course a bottle of white wine chilling in the depths over the side in a bag just waiting for an unexpected guest to stop by is always a welcome reward.

In winter months a boom tent can be a blessing as they can turn your cockpit into a large porch so to speak. They keep the rain out of the boat when you want to leave the hatch open, and still offer a good place to go topside should you desire. If high winds develop, you may want to take it down, but it's easy to put back up at anytime. Four or five grommets on each edge can allow you to stretch it out with bungees to your upright stanchions. This will help to keep it taut in most wind and weather conditions. You should take it down if it snows, this is a condition often encountered in the northwest.

Many power boats have an overhang from their fly bridge. This is a blessing in disguise for those who want to spend time topside and in some degree of shade. Yet in the winter months, money spent on adding a cockpit cover from the overhang, down to the edges of your cockpit, will be well worth while. If you don't have a fly bridge, there are other ways of providing a cover for your stern cockpit in the winter months. Perhaps you could add two or more floor flanges from your local hardware store.

Floor flanges are threaded for various sizes of pipe, giving you a choice in the amount of strength you need to support an overhead cover. It would then be a simple matter of building a frame work out of galvanized pipe to support your winter canvas cover. If you prefer something more aesthetic, of course use stainless steel. Either way you choose to go, the frame work can be removed for the summer weather and cruising.

BAGGY WRINKLES

With baggy wrinkles on my shrouds I've had many people ask, *"What are those bottle-brush-looking things on your upper shrouds for?"*

Not only do they look nautical, but they do indeed serve a very useful purpose. Look at your sails when underway and you will notice black marks, or dark stains on them where they chafe against the shrouds.

Baggy wrinkles have been with us for a very long time. You don't see them much anymore, especially on boats in the inland waterways. However most cruising sailors are well aware of the protection they offer sails on long passages. The best part is that you can make your own baggy wrinkles quite easily.

The life span of baggy wrinkles can vary, but the last ones I made were still in good shape after four years of service, a little darker in color, and not quite as fluffy, but still doing their job.

The main requirement for making baggy wrinkles is patience. Two others are hemp rope and Sisal twine. Manila rope is the best you can use. Anything else will crumble, rot, or just plain droop in a relatively short time.

A one-inch diameter piece of hemp rope will have four main strands, each made up of a multitude of smaller strands of fiber. Cut the strands of hemp line into six-inch pieces. Eighteen of these six-inch pieces will be enough to produce a baggy wrinkle about twelve to fifteen inches long. You'll have to guess how much one-inch rope to purchase, but no matter because you will always have a use for the remnants at some time in the future.

Find two posts about eight to ten feet apart. It's possible to use the fore-triangle between your forestay and a cleat on your mainmast, or between your mizzen mast and your backstay.

Cut a piece of Sisal twine fourteen feet long and put the ends together. Tie them into an overhand knot about six inches from the ends. Now tie another knot the same distance in from the other end of the loop as shown in the drawing.

In the process of making these baggy wrinkles, I've found that using a couple of Bungee-cords from the posts to the twine keeps it taut, and this is something you want to do.

Using one of the four strand pieces you cut at a six-inch length, break it down into separate fibers, and put them into place on the suspended Sisal twine. To do this, you loop them out and around the outside edges of the loop of twine, then tuck the ends between the two strands of twine, and pointed towards the end you are working from.

When in place, push them to the end, packing each one tightly against the one before. You continue this process until you cannot push any more onto the twine.

I suggest that if you are putting the baggy wrinkles up at the spreaders, you start about seven inches above the spreader tip. This will put the end of your finished baggy wrinkle abut seven inches below the spreader tip. Or, you can put a complete baggy wrinkle above and below the spreader tips.

Tie the six-inch loop onto the shroud, and spiral wrap the twine-hemp around the shroud, working from top to bottom. When you reach the end, simply tie it off.

As you answer questions from others, you'll feel like one of the, 'Old Salts.'

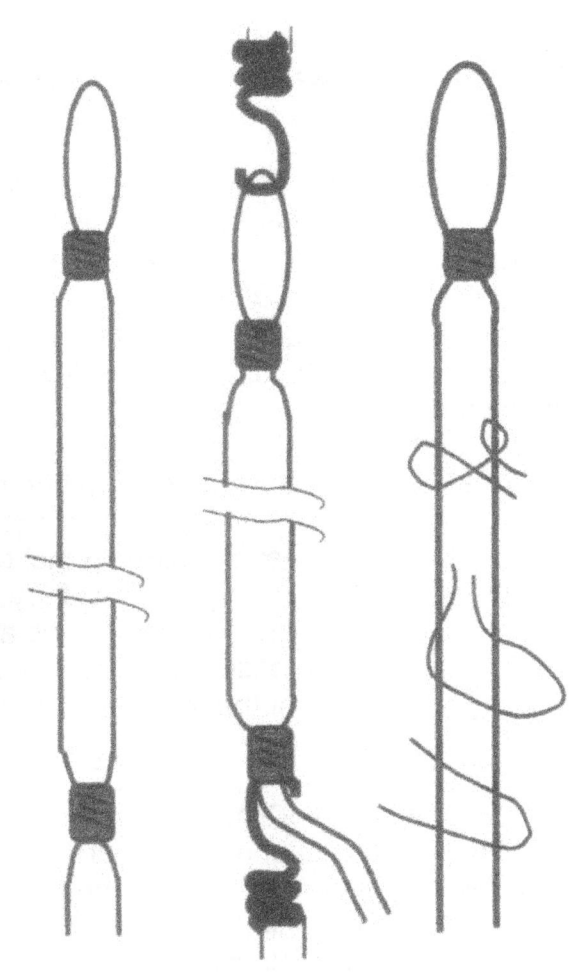

BOW ROLLERS

I found myself with an anchor problem when I purchased a new Plow anchor. My present bow roller allowed the Plow anchor fluke to bang against the hull in rough weather, and this was a situation I wanted to avoid.

This presented two problems, finding a bow roller long enough to do the job, and at a price that did not require payments for the extensive credit card bill that would follow. Because of the difficulty in finding one long enough, I decided to manufacture my own. It was not a simple job, but the following process worked well.

I went to a sheet metal shop and had them cut a piece of 300 grade, corrosion resistant aluminum for me. I chose a piece sixteen by thirty-six inches, cut from quarter-inch stock. After it was cut they bent it for me into a channel with six inch sides and a four-inch wide base. The base width you use will be dependent on the width of the roller you use on your boat.

After measuring the boat and the anchor once more, I cut the aluminum channel to the proper size with an electric jig saw and using a metal cutting blade. A half round file helped in smoothing all of the edges. Next I drilled a hole for a stainless steel bolt to accommodate a boat trailer roller.

The roller was fastened in place using the bolt with washers and an aircraft style lock nut. This left only the mounting of the new bow roller on my foredeck.

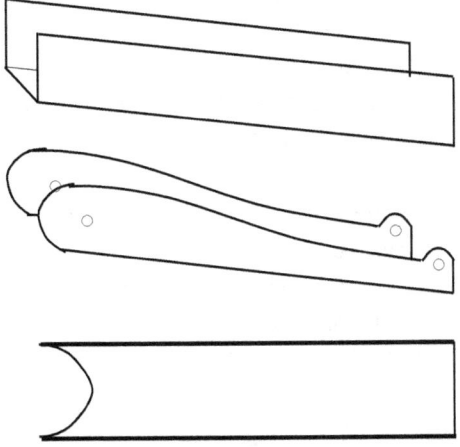

CURE THAT DRAGGING HATCH

Over the years the main hatch cover on our sailboat began to drag and become hard to open, especially if you were inside where it was not as easy to push the hatch forward from below deck. I began to inspect the hatch and found that where it was riding on top of the coach roof, it was wearing a channel into the fiber glass and wearing out both surfaces.

I found a simple and inexpensive solution for the problem. I found some cloth webbing at a surplus store in our area, though it was longer than I needed, the width was nearly perfect and I already had some five minute two part epoxy.

Topside, I removed the wooden plugs covering the mounting screws for the hatch guides and retainers. You want to do this carefully to avoid damaging the wood around the plug holes, but you can drill a quarter inch hole into the plugs, this gives you a hole to help in removing the plugs. You can replace the plugs later with plugs you can get from your chandlery. With this done, the guides were removed and the hatch cover lifted off, and turned upside down on top of the cabin.

If the grooves in your coach roof are of a depth that concerns you, you can fill them with a Gel Coat patch kit purchased at nearly any chandlery. On the coach roof, where the hatch cover slides back and forth, sand the area where the webbing will be placed.

You have to make a choice now, do you want a full length piece of webbing on each side, or three or four shorter pieces. These are used to make the hatch slide open and closed easily.

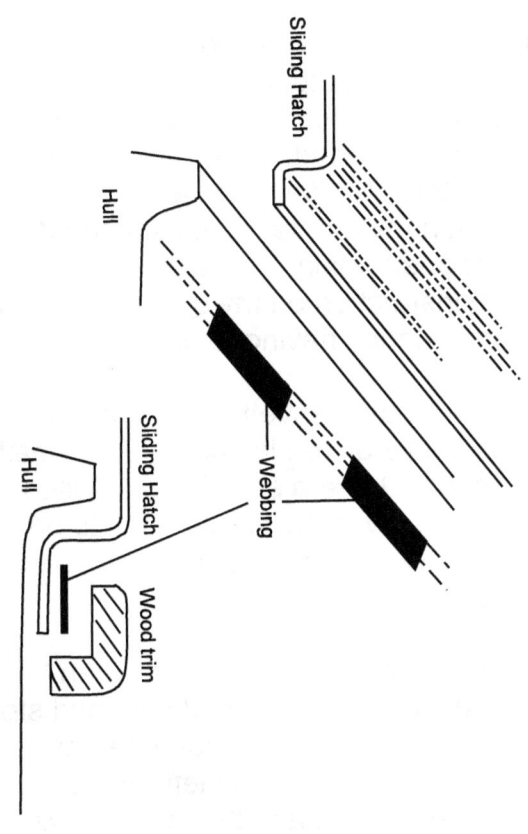

HATCH BOARDS, OR DOORS

When you spend a great deal of time aboard a sailboat small enough to have hatch boards, you get tired of the constant lifting them out, and then putting them back into place every time you enter or exit the boat.

One day I looked with envy at some fabricated doors at a boat dealership, doors that replaced the hatch boards so that you could just swing them open or closed as needed. I only looked long enough to see the price tag of several hundred dollars plus, then my mental wallet slammed shut and would not open again. This was when my mind began construction on my own set of doors, and for far less money having to be spent.

In my case I wanted to leave the bottom hatch board in place while at sea in case of foul weather. Therefore, I couldn't use a set of doors built on a slip in framework. My doors would have to be independent of each other, yet easily removed, or put into place as needed.

The intention was to build doors that, when I was aboard, I could lift the hatch boards out and store them away until needed. Then place the doors onto a set of lift off hinges until I left the boat again. The materials to make these doors will change with each boat owner's taste in wood. For my doors I used the following items. The cost was less than one hundred dollars.

12 feet of 1.0" X 3.0" Red Mahogany
2 custom cut pieces of 3/8" plastic
4 Chrome lift off hinges
1 tube of caulking, and some glue

A table saw and a router are very handy for this job, and you start by taking very careful measurements.

My boat has teak trim on both sides of the hatch. These are used for retaining the manufactured hatch boards that came with the boat. I used these to mount the lower one half of the split hinges, for both the upper and lower hinges.

Cut all of the wood pieces with mitered corners and at the required angles as needed. By mitering the corners you add a greater surface for the glued corner joints, which adds strength to the joints.

You must decide how the center of the doors are to come together. If they just meet in the center, you may have a leak when you don't want one. If, on the other hand, if you overlap them, you can avoid most air and water leaks. You can even use an insulating strip where they overlap.

I drilled all of my corners to accept a long screw to further strengthen the corners and to pull them together even tighter, then I covered the screw head with a nice wooden plug. I also cut a 1/2" slot into the middle of the inner edge of each piece to accept the plastic panel, and this was caulked just before the plastic panel was put into place during the final assembly of each door.

With the door assembly finished, you can fit the upper half of the hinges onto the door halves, and make sure they are in line with the edges of the hatch wood trim. If they are not in line, the door may bind when opening or closing.

1. Carefully cut all of the pieces of wood for the door according to the measurements you made of the hatch.

2. Determine the depth of the groove into the wood for the plastic panel, and cut this groove with a router or table saw. The width of this groove will be determined by the thickness of the plastic panel.

3. Fit all of the pieces together temporarily for each separate door, including the plastic panels.

4. Drill the holes for the corner screw locations.

5. Take the temporary assembly apart and when you are certain all of the parts fit together correctly, you can caulk the grooves and reassemble the door halves together. When the caulk has set up you can trim the excess with a knife.

These doors can last the lifetime of your vessel if made correctly. They also offer many hours of free passage to and from inside the boat. Varnish on red mahogany makes a good looking finish, but of course you may prefer paint depending on your choice of wood used.

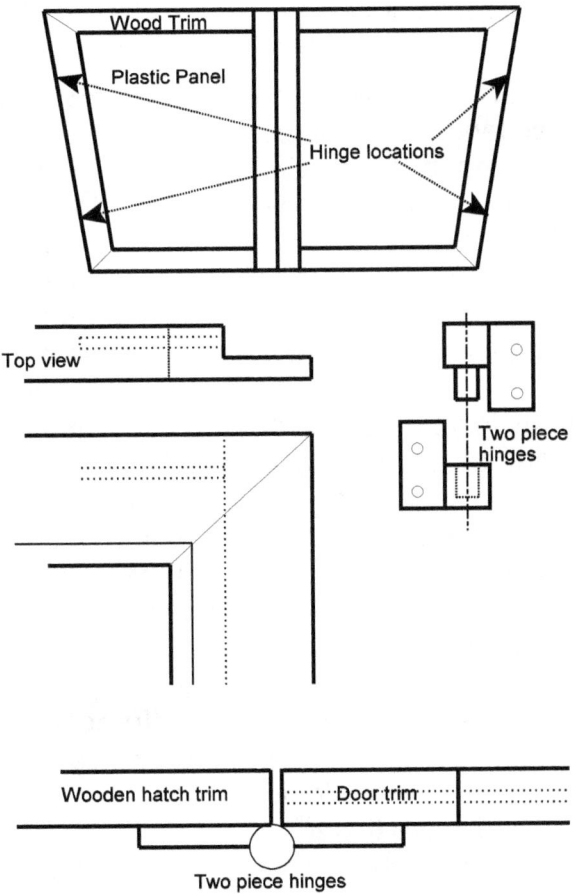

NOISES IN THE NIGHT

Quite by accident I found that a simple piece of plastic pipe would tell me the conditions that were taking place topside at night. The message was either I could go back to sleep, or if I had to get up to have a look around.

I found that if you place a piece of 4.0" PVC pipe, cut in half length wise across your foredeck and under your anchor line, it will convey a lot of information to you should you wake during the night. There are of course, other noises in the night, but for the moment I'll try to explain the noises concerning the PVC pipe on your foredeck, then I'll explain how to build it and put it in place.

As you lay in your vee-berth you can hear the anchor line as it passes over the PVC pipe, especially if it is tight. If you hear a short, 'Stretch' noise, then it remains quiet for a length of time, finally to hear the 'Slack' noise, as the boat begins to sail on the anchor line to its next location, you're probably okay.

The time period between the two different noises is the time the boat has stopped moving away from the anchor, which is holding the boat in its chosen position, and when it starts going the other way. When it again reaches its limit, you will hear the familiar 'Stretch' noise, then again the 'Slack' noise. If they are consistent, you can probably go back to sleep.

If, however, you hear, 'Stretch - retch - etch - tch - ch,' then it's quiet, you may be sailing a long ways. Finally the good news, 'Slack - lack - ack - ch.'

This tells you two things. One is that your anchor is holding, two is that perhaps you should have a look around topside. If the wind has picked up enough, it may warrant paying out some more anchor rode to give you an additional safety factor.

If, when you wake up, all is quiet, odds are all is well and there is no wind. If, you wake up and hear waves lapping on one side of the hull and it seems odd, you should probably have a look around topside. This is often a clue that you may be dragging the anchor, and the wind is pushing you sideways.

Trusting your anchor also reflects on how well you sleep while anchored out. You will read recommended anchor sizes depending on the boat length. These might say an 18 pound anchor is suitable for a boat from 24 to 31 feet in length, often depending on whether it is a sailboat or a power boat. You will also read that a 20 pound anchor is good for boats up to 32 feet.

There is just no way in the world I would sleep well at night with anything less than a 35 pound plow, with 40 feet of 3/8" chain between the anchor and the anchor rode on my 30 foot sailboat. I don't know how this will work for anything other than Nylon line, and if you use all chain rode, you might try this trick under your Nylon snubber line. But, if you have all chain rode, you sleep well at night anyway.

Once you become accustomed to listening to the noises in the night, you can hear the tide turn, or currents around the boat change. I kid you not, sleep well.

The length, and end slots, will depend on your particular needs.

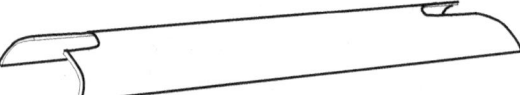

The size diameter of the plastic pipe will depend on your particular needs.

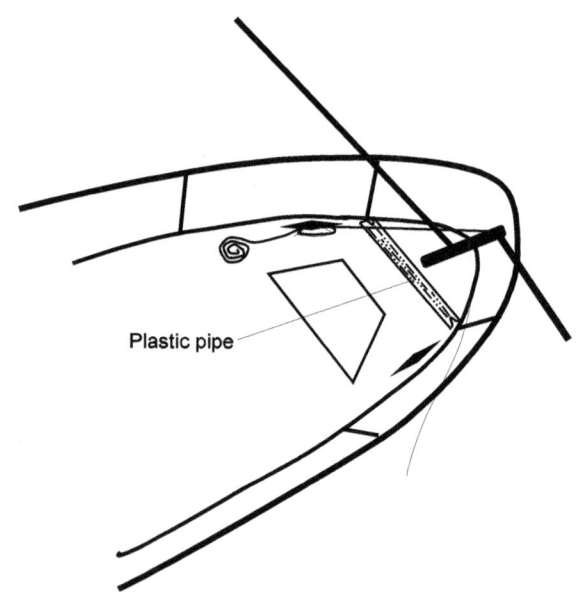

Plastic pipe

OUTBOARD MOTOR BRACKETS

Lyn and I were a long way from any source of engine parts when the head gasket blew out on our inboard engine. There was little if any wind, and now we were without an auxiliary engine as well. Before the engine quit entirely we were able to limp into an anchorage on the north side of Lopez Island, but once the engine was shut down we knew we were going nowhere under power. Fortunately, we were towing our Zodiac inflatable with a nine horse power outboard motor.

Luckily, the next morning, I found a boater living in a cabin just above the shoreline. After a few minutes of explanatory conversation, Mr. Bishop gave me the keys to his car and said softly, with a knowing twinkle in his eyes, "It's too old to steal, so just use it." In using his telephone book, I located a chandlery on the other side of the island. At the chandlery I found a good outboard engine bracket that locks in the up, or down, position with a flick of a small lever.

Back onboard our boat I went to work. Using our dinghy off the starboard quarter, I drilled the holes required for mounting the outboard motor bracket. When the bracket was mounted and the motor attached, our nine-horsepower outboard motor would just drop into the water at the proper depth. I did find that with the bracket in the up position, the propeller would still drag in the water. To prevent wear on the bearings I locked the motor in gear, thus stopping the prop rotation.

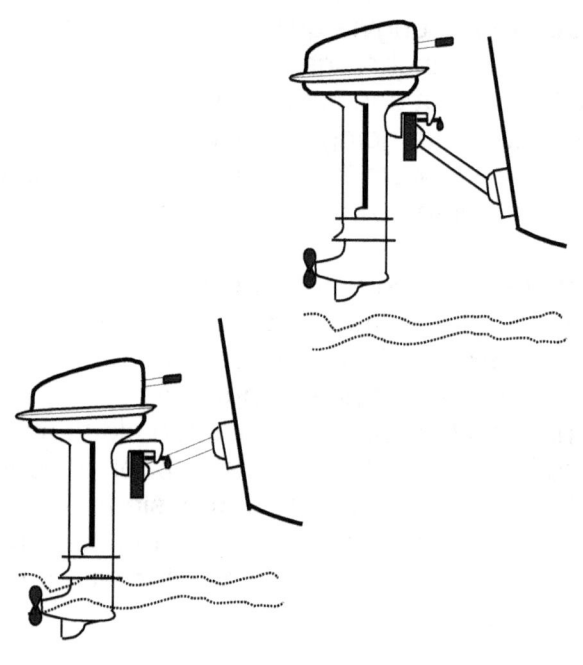

PUSHPIT GATE

I can't remember how many times I had to crawl over the stern pushpit and climb carefully down the ladder mounted on the back of the boat and into our dinghy trailing off the stern. The real problem being that my legs are not long enough to provide enough clearance to go over the rail without some personal concerns. I decided there had to be a better way. It would be much easier and less painful if I simply built a removable gate into the stern rail.

To do this you'll need a tubing cutter, or a hacksaw to cut the stainless steel tubing, and with the proper blade. Then, depending on the type of fitting you purchase, you may also need drill bits for stainless steel, and a small bottle of cutting oil. Drilling stainless steel requires drilling slowly while applying a few drops of cutting oil to the end of the drill bit while it bites into the metal.

You will need to purchase two, 'Tee' fittings that have a flat section with a bolt hole. And two tubing-to-eye fittings. Or, two Tee fittings and four tubing-to-eye fittings. I think the first combination is the better. These are often used for railing and Bimini tops.

Pick a convenient section between two upright stanchions. Cut both stanchions where they intersect with the rail, and using the Tee fitting as a guide, cut the rail to allow the Tee fitting to be pushed in place.

This will join the rail and stanchion together again. Now insert one of the tubing-to-eye fittings into one end of the remaining piece of railing and one into one of the Tee fittings now in place at the railing stanchion intersection.

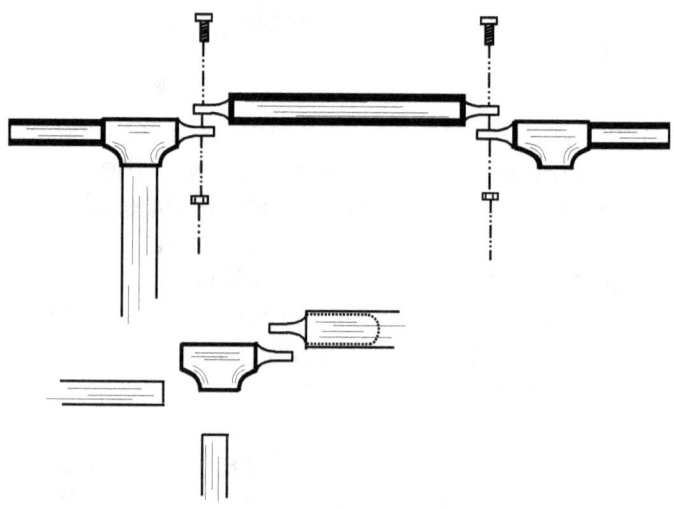

SIMPLE SHOWERS

My wife is one of those who want her hair washed nearly every day, with which I have no problem as long as we have the water. Except our first boat didn't have a shower stall arrangement in which she could wash her hair. I'm one of those lucky guys who happens to have a wife who likes to travel on the boat, so I do whatever it takes to keep her happy and I spoil her.

I found a way to make a shower setup that worked quite well, it didn't use a lot of water, and wasn't too inconvenient.

Go to a garden supply shop and purchase a three gallon plastic weed spray container. This is the type that you can pump pressure up in the tank by using the handle as a pump. These usually have a spray nozzle on the end of the hose, but you are going to remove that one and replace it with a replacement hose and nozzle that have a hand controlled spray nozzle for a kitchen sink.

You will also need a couple of small hose clamps to secure your new hose onto the spout from which you removed the original hose.

When you begin to use this new portable shower system you'll have to experiment, but you may find that filling it about 1/3 full of hot water, then adding cold water to suit your needs works best.

The shower tank can be left standing on deck while in use, and easily pumping up the tank pressure when it gets too low.

You may have to renew the pressure once or twice for each person's use, but that will be about all there is to it. And yes, three gallons of water is just about right for two people.

As for a shower stall, if you don't have one, buy a plastic tarpaulin, one of those blue ones will work well. It will offer sufficient privacy. Get a size that is convenient to use in your boat's cockpit. On a sailboat this can be hung from your main or mizzen boom. A power boat will require a different kind of arrangement.

You may want to form it into a squared area, and it can be held in this shape by using some wooden dowels going across to the opposite corners. On the side where the corners meet, this can be used as the doorway in and out of the shower.

Once you are finished with your shower each time, it can be stored in a locker by merely folding it up, the shower tank should be de-pressurized until it is needed again.

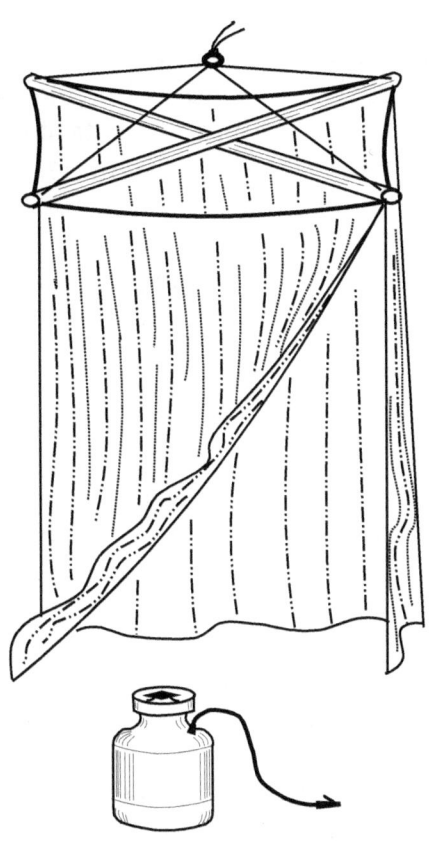

BELOW DECK

COOK STOVE REPLACEMENT
One of the first things Lyn did when we went aboard our future boat home was to look the stove over, a natural response for anyone who may have to use one of these standard equipment boating stoves for an extended period. And, her immediate examination came with a suggestion.

"We should think about replacing this stove." Which, when properly deciphered, means, 'We will get a new one.'

We began by frequenting the larger chandlers in our area, looking for the best price, and the price of a new stainless steel stove with an oven was, to put it mildly, frightening. Yet, there wasn't really a choice in the matter, we were going to get a new stove somehow.

Armed with the exact measurements of the opening where the new stove would reside, and they are different from top to bottom, I went to a recreational vehicle supplier, and inquired as to stove prices. They provided me with some brochures that included drawings and the dimension specifications.

Back onboard the boat we compared our findings with the space we had available, and settled on the 'MAGIC CHEF' propane stove. It has four burners, a nice large oven and a pilot light you can turn on, or off, at your discretion .

The price was very well received at slightly less than half that of the stainless steel stove.

The stove fit the space we had perfectly. The same propane gas line that was connected to our previous stove could be used for this one. It was connected as the new stove was put into place.

You will find those that argue that a stove produced for the recreational vehicle will not survive in the harsh environment of the marine world. We used this stove for many, many years and it never showed any signs of rusting, corroding, or any other kind of malfunction due to being on board a sailboat in saltwater conditions continually.

HEATING STOVES

We had purchased a small stainless steel heating stove some time ago, but until recently we had not used it to heat the boat. When the time came to use it, we were anchored out in a protected cove. The nest morning a chill indicated it was time to light a fire in that nice little stove.

I'd mounted the stove on a tile covered backboard to keep it from getting the bulkhead too hot. As it turns out there wasn't much to worry about from that stove. Oh, the sheet metal got hotter than a furnace door, but as soon as the fire's flames died away, everything was soon cold again. The stove was a disappointment, it did not hold any heat, and I knew I had to find a way to retain the stove's

I contacted a local rock and tile shop where I obtained pieces of Terra Cotta tiles. These tiles are so hard that I had the shop cut them for me to my dimensions.

The next step was to disassemble the stove. I removed the hardware that keeps the stove's outer protective sheet metal in place. With it still surrounding the stove, I slipped the two larger pieces of tile in along side of the stove. One on each side. The smaller odd piece was placed in the back behind the fire box. A smaller piece yet was to be placed on top of the unit when it was reassembled. There are brackets on each side to support the outer protective shield and the pieces of tile go next to the skin of the stove, but in between these supports. In this manner they still support the outer shield and they retain the tiles in their required areas as well.

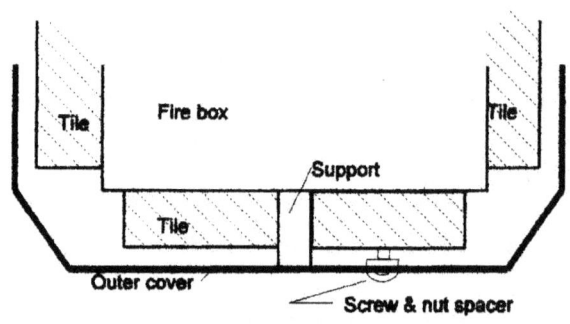

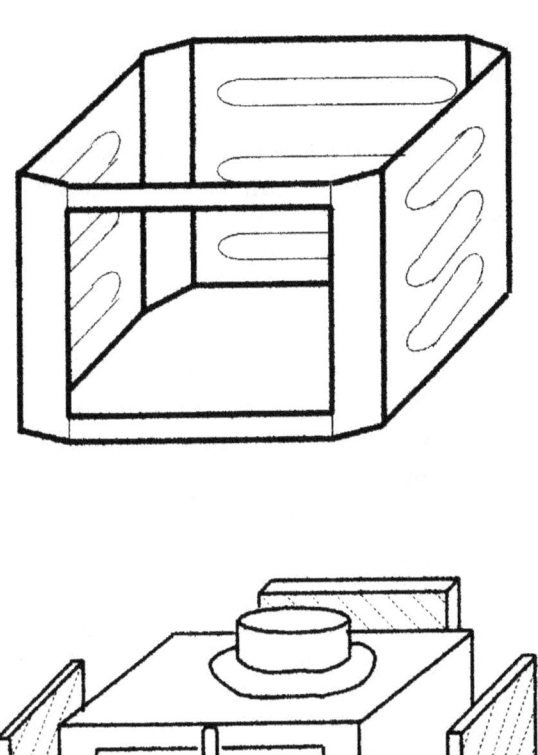

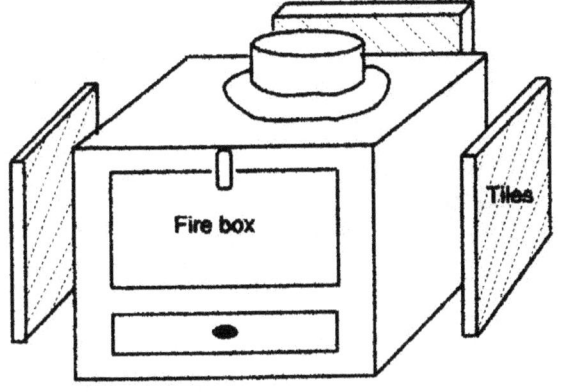

ICE BOX DILEMMA

Seems odd that a boat's interior designer would put an icebox in a location where you had to reach over a potentially hot stove to retrieve an item for a meal while fixing the meal. Yet, in our sailboat, that is exactly what happened.

My wife, a buxom lass, turned the heat up on me to find a cure for the situation, and the cure was to use the factory ice box as a long term storage unit. you know, for canned goods, rice, flour, sugar etc. So now the problem was what to do for an icebox?

I decided that the best place to put an icebox was in a location presently being occupied by a two-drawer cabinet assembly to the left, and aft of the new propane stove we had put in. I could move the drawers from the assembly to a new location so that they could still be utilized as storage space.

I began to ask around in the marine industry for information concerning a manufacturer of iceboxes in today's world. None was found, but a savvy auto-parts sales clerk suggested looking in a J.C. Whitney catalog. I don't know how long this company has been around, but I'd guess it started about the same time as Studebaker wagons.

I found exactly what I needed, but since then J.C. Whitney has added new items to the list, and some of these may work better for you than just an icebox.

They have small refrigerators that have very low DC power requirements. You can go online to *www.jcwhitney.com* and order a free catalog.

With an icebox at the ready, I had to cut an opening to accommodate the new icebox in the fiberglass, as it is larger than the factory unit of drawers that was held in place by four large screws. Once removed, the only problem I encountered was some of the foam insulation that was a part of the original icebox built in the boat at the factory. I simply gouged out some of this foam to let my new icebox to fit in place.

I marked out my needed opening on the fiberglass surface with a marker pen, but before you do this you must consider which side of the icebox, or refrigerator, that you want the door hinges so the door can open. This is an option, and if you don't plan accordingly you may find you don't have enough room for the door to swing open properly.

With these decisions made, I cut the opening using a jigsaw. Be sure to wear a white dust mask. This left enough room for the mounting screws on each side and for the door to open. It also left my fire extinguisher in its original location.

As I pushed the new icebox into place, Lyn pulled on a small piece of line that pulled the icebox drain tube down into the bilge area where it would be connected to a storage tank, and the melt water could be pumped out at any time.

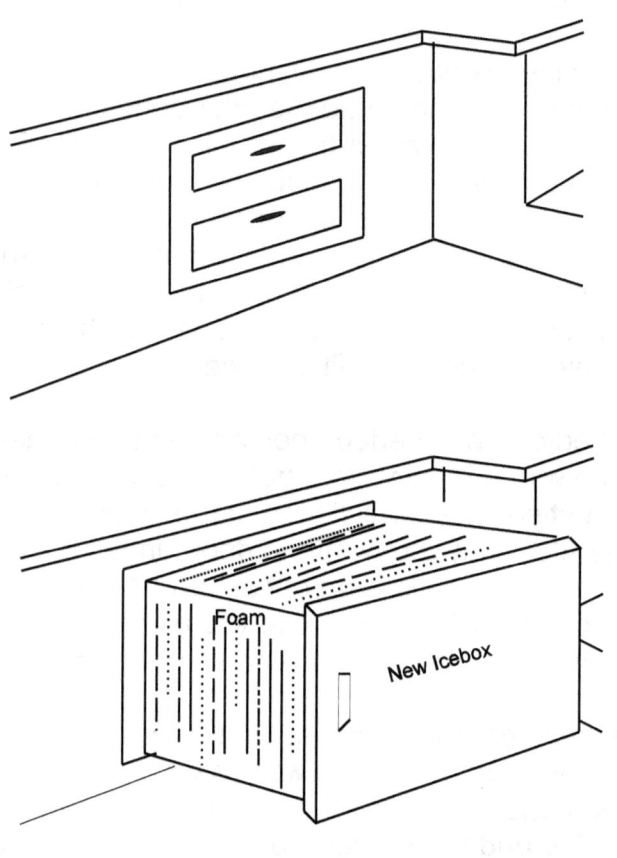

TABLE MODIFICATION

When Lyn and I purchased our sailboat, 'Itchy Feet,' it had a table standing on end and fastened against the forward bulkhead in the main salon. These are commonly placed in a space between the edge of the settee and that same forward bulkhead with a leg or two used to support the outside edge. Supposedly they are used as a large bed. I say large bed because it may be similar to a double size bed, but isn't.

This unsightly arrangement wasn't a problem for us because we rarely have overnight guests onboard. Well, perhaps an occasional grandchild, or on a rare occurrence, a mother in-law, but any of the above can sleep in the quarter berth.

I wanted to put a small heating stove on the forward bulkhead wall in question, yet I still needed a table. At times I knew I would need the advantage of the original size table, but I could use a smaller table most of the time and one that didn't take as much space when it was set up in place.

The solution was to cut our existing table in half and keep the other half as a bed filler, much like a table leaf. I found the solution by purchasing a set of trestle table extension slides. These are used on some tables to pull the table open and insert the center leaf when the table needs to be bigger. I removed the original metal table fastening supports from the forward bulkhead and moved them down two and a half inches. Doing so, would maintain the original table height. Then from the end of the original table I removed the pieces that slipped into the metal wall brackets from the edge of the table and I fastened them to the bottom of the new table slides.

When you do this you must be sure the screws do not go through the wood so far as to interfere with the movement of the sliding portion of the extension. Also, these are normally made of a hard wood so it is wise to pre-drill any holes needed to keep from splitting the wood. When you fasten the other halves of the slides to the table remember to place them the same distance apart as the remaining brackets you have mounted on the wall.

Finished, I hung the table on the wall, dropped the original leg down to the cabin sole and stood back to admire my new, but shorter table. The other half of the table is kept at the aft end of the quarter berth. When we need it, we simply pull out the short table, and set the other half behind it, as you would place a leaf in your table at home.

There can be a problem of keeping your short table against the wall, I mean it's now on slides, right?

I fastened two small eye-bolts, one on each side, into the bottom of the table, but out of sight, then I put two screen door hook latches on the wall.

These of course, are the kind that have a piece of sheet metal for a locking device to keep them from dropping out of the eye-bolts.

You may have to place a small wood strip near the outside edge of the part of the table you use as a table leaf to keep it from sliding sideways. You might also check your table for solidity by pushing down on one of the outside corners. If it tilts, you may have to place a strip of wood along the top edge of the table against the wall when it is set in place. This can be done by screwing it to the wall, and leaving enough room to tilt the table downwards to remove it as you normally would to get it out of the way.

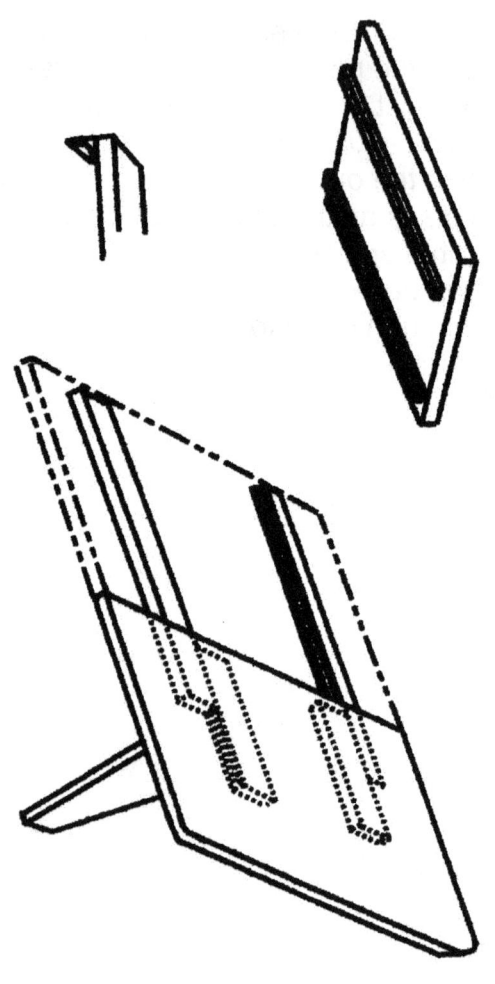

PRIVACY CURTAINS

You're out walking on the docks on a pleasant evening, and you happen to pass a boat with lights on below. You look inside, but it's not an intentional look, it just happens. If there had been curtains, you would never have looked, and therein lies the problem. Without curtains on your portals, there is little privacy while at the dock.

Curtains are easily available if you don't mind drilling holes in your boat. I for one, do not like drilling holes anywhere in my boat, and avoid doing this whenever possible. However, my dear wife found a way to make custom curtains without the need for holes.

Find a craft store in your area and purchase some plastic canvas used in needlepoint craft projects. No you don't have to be a gifted artist, all you need do is take a few measurements and be able to use a pair of scissors. This stuff is stiff, but flexible enough for this use, and it is a great sight barrier from the outside, but not from the inside. That is, you can see out, but you can't see in.

With eight portals in our boat, Lyn started with a piece of number ten mesh, twenty-four inches by thirty-six inches. Most portals will have a half inch of space between the glass and the lip of the portal's edge. In this case this is good because you cut the plastic canvas to fit inside each portal's opening.

I'd advise you to cut one of the larger pieces first, then if you make an error, it can still be used on one of the smaller locations.

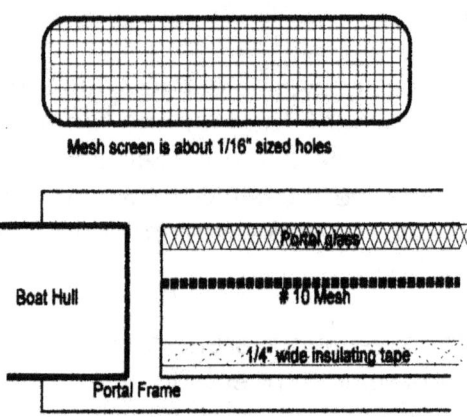

VEE BIRTH STORAGE LOCKER

You know how you have to have that filler board in place to make your vee berth into a larger bed so you and your sweetheart can snuggle at night. Yes the same filler board that covers up the step the manufacturer built into this spot so that you could get into bed as if it was only used as a single bunk on each side.

And you know all of that wasted space under that filler board that you just stack up stuff that you have to go through each time you need something that is there somewhere. Well, why not use it to your advantage. With a little careful measuring, a small amount of plywood and a finish of your choosing, it can become a very useful storage area. You can make a simple wall that goes across the opening, so that when you lift the filler board, you have access to the area below, or you can get a little fancier by adding a shelf and openings in the front for more storage diversity.

I used a scroll saw to cut the holes for the false drawer fronts in my piece of plywood, top and bottom, and the bottom edge of each was cut at an angle on the inside to help lock the cover in place against the curvature of the hull. On the outside I glued and used small finish nails, to fasten molding all around the edges of the holes I'd cut, as if they were picture frames.

Using the molding helps add a finishing touch regardless of how straight your cutting line turns out. Here's a brief drawing of how the side view would look, and the construction of the locking latch would be built. The latch is made out of a drawer pull handle, but with two nuts and a small piece of sheet metal to go on the inside.

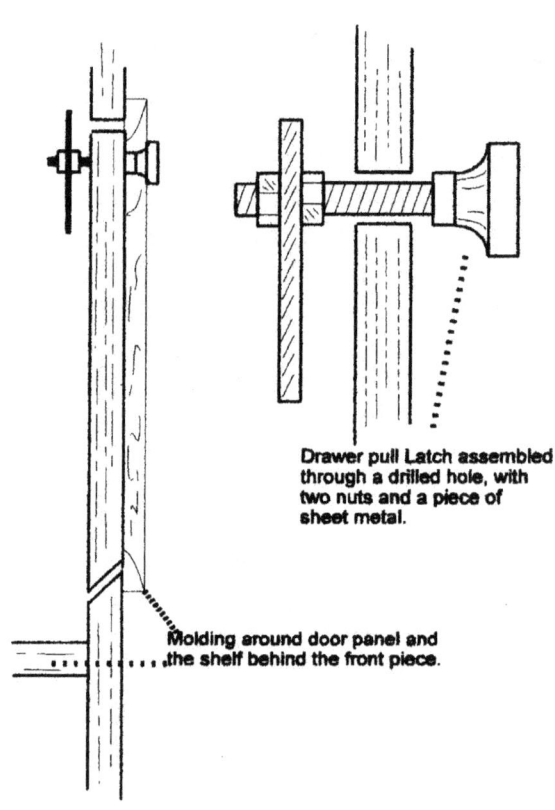

Drawer pull Latch assembled through a drilled hole, with two nuts and a piece of sheet metal.

Molding around door panel and the shelf behind the front piece.

ELECTRICAL

RESURRECTED AUTO-PILOTS
Having purchased boat number nine in my life, I found the autopilot that was left aboard did not work. It would run accept to run from a full Port or Starboard turn. It would stop at nothing in between.

I took the unit home, then called the Autohelm factory in New Hampshire. Unfortunately, they informed me that the unit I possessed could no longer be repaired. With factory repair options gone I took it upon myself to open the autopilot case to have a look inside. I found the flux-gate compass unit was loose inside the case. However, after an unsuccessful attempt to lock the compass unit in its proper place, I realized I had a useless piece of equipment.

As I mulled the situation over, a simple solution came to mind. If I modified the autopilot, I could have a very useful electric steering device. It took almost an hour of easy effort, but at least I had something that could be used to steer the boat from anywhere on the boat. Topside, or below deck.

Now, with my boat engine running at idle, I can walk forward to the bow, or to a higher position than the cockpit well, and watch for rocks or sandbars when entering tight passages. With a long electrical cord and a switch on my end, I can steer the boat from any position on the boat by using the converted autopilot.

The switch is normally in the off position, but it is a double throw, double pole switch. This allows the user to move the switch from the 'OFF' position, to either side of the switch. One side represents the Port direction, the other side is for the Starboard. The parts you'll need, and the steps to making the modification, are as follows. However, you may have to inquire as to the current part numbers.

Radio Shack:
Cat. No. 275-709 Momentary, center off, auto flip switch.

www.mouser.com
538-23041 4-pin in-line socket with strain relief.
538-13041 4-pin in-line plug with strain relief.

A length of four conductor 18 gauge stranded wire, of your chosen length, to reach the locations from which you want to operate your modified auto-pilot.

1. Remove any screws holding the compass rose adjustment plate, and any accompanying pieces onto the auto-pilot housing.

2. Remove any screws from the housing that hold the unit together. You might want to keep these in a re-sealable plastic bag until you're ready to re-assemble the unit.

3. If your unit has a swivel base for mounting purposes, it can be temporarily removed to make your work easier.

4. Inside the case you will find a round cylinder, (in most cases), to which the compass rose may have been attached, and contains the flux gate compass, or magnetic direction finder. This is often the culprit that has failed, and can be removed from the auto-pilot case.

5. If there is a return spring attached to the drive screw mechanism, it can be removed as it will no longer be needed.

6. A circuit board, and you should have one, can be removed, but make note of any wires going to the drive motor. These leads from the motor, (two), should be left as long as possible, but removed from the circuit board.

7. Should it so happen that you have a wind-vane attachment, it too can be removed as can any associated wiring.

8. Many models have a toggle switch for turning the power to the unit, on/off. If it does not have one, you may want to install one for power control, or safety reasons if nothing else.

9. You will need to drill holes for any parts added, such as a toggle switch if you don't already have one, and the female in-line socket. This last hole

may require some fitting handiwork on your part. Be certain, any holes you put in for equipment you're adding, will not interfere with other interior components.

!0. Possibly the best way to mount the female in-line socket into the case, will be to use an epoxy glue.

11. The wiring diagram supplied was used in my particular Auto-Helm, and may work as a guide for your own purposes.

12. Applying 12 Volt current to the center terminals of the switch, will allow battery and ground to flow to the corresponding terminals on either side of the switch. The wires, that are soldered across the switch, in an X pattern, will change the direction of current flow to the drive motor, thus reversing its direction. Or, the Port and Starboard steering directions.

13. Once you find out which direction is which, on your switch setup, you may want to mark them somehow, as to 'Port,' and 'Starboard.'

14. I made a mold around my steering toggle switch with a small can of 'Bondo'. Yes, the same stuff used to fix dents in your car. This allows you to make a watertight unit, but do not use an epoxy resin as it can flood the switch and it will cease to function.

15. You can reassemble the unit using a bit of bee's wax, or silicone sealant on the joints, but you should put it together with the intention of getting back inside at some point.

NOTE:
The difference between electrical motors is often misunderstood. An AC current motor is common in many household appliances. Reversing the electrical current to this motor will only result in disaster. However, a DC motor is most often used in boats, automobiles, and Recreational Vehicles, is another matter. Reversing the electrical current in this kind of motor will result in its running the other direction. Step motors are another whole world and will not be discussed here.

TOOLS
The tools you use may vary from user to user, but the more commonly used will be.
      Long nose pliers
      Wire cutters
      Screw drivers, perhaps phillips and a flat blade
      Soldering iron

The more common items needed other than the parts, can be:
      Solder
      RTV sealant
      Bee's wax
      Electrical tape, *or heat shrink depending*

> *upon your personal desires for covering wire terminals if at all.*

Bondo, marine or auto type can be used
Five minute epoxy

One last item. The particular Auto-pilot you have may not be identical to the one illustrated here. However, the information in this section should serve as a guide to your attempting to covert nearly any defunct Auto-pilot. If it is not responding and you know it's headed for the dumpster, what have you got to lose.

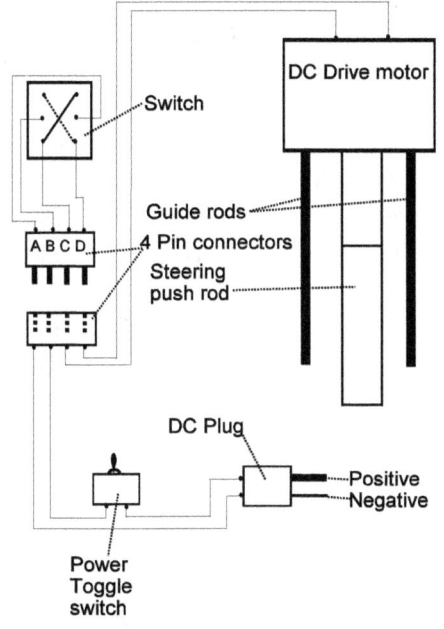

Simulated wiring diagram for auto-pilot

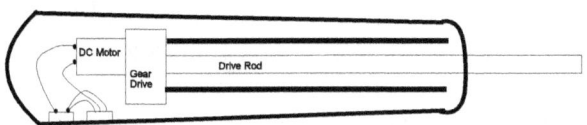

TELEVISION ANTENNA

Of course we watch television while we spend time on the boat, I mean the soaps go on forever and so do some of the characters. We use a small color television that operates on 12 VDC, or on 120 VAC, the problem, of course, is in getting the signal.

You can purchase an antenna for a few hundred dollars, or you can simply build your own antenna that will work well under most conditions. And you can build it quite cheaply, and quite easily.

The size of the copper tubing you will need, will depend on your own choice, but I'd recommend you use tubing at least 3/8" inside diameter. The items you will need are as follows:

1. Two pieces of 3/8" copper tubing, with an inside diameter, of eighteen inches in length.

2. A piece of wood 1.0" X 4.0" X 24.0" unless you decide you would like the antenna to fold in the middle for easier storage when not in use. If this is your decision, you will need two pieces of wood 1.0" X 2.0" X 24.0" in length.

3. A length of Coax television cable long enough to reach from the location you wish to mount the antenna, to the area where you want to keep the TV set. If possible, purchase a cable that already has the connectors installed on the cable ends.

If not, you can install them yourself with a cheap crimping tool.

4. A 1/4" eye-bolt, with a nut and a washer.

5. A 1/4" blind-nut.

6. A length of piano hinge, if needed for the easier storage option, about 15.0" long.

7. Eight #8 X 1-1/2" wood screws.

8. A 1/4" eye-bolt, with a nut and a washer.

9. A 1/4" blind-nut.

10. A length of piano hinge, if needed for the easier storage option, about 15.0" long.

11. Eight #8 X 1-1/2" wood screws.

Start by bending the two pieces of copper tubing into semicircles. A tree trunk, or a light pole, works well for maintaining the radius without kinking the tubing in the bending process. A sailboat mast may be too small in diameter, but may work if you take your time and be patient. A trick that may help is to fill the tubing with sand before you start. This will add strength to the tubing during the bending.

The ends will come together when bent correctly. When the bending is completed, remove the sand if you used this method, then flatten the ends for about 1-1/2". When you lay the half circle of tubing down on a flat surface, the flattened ends should be vertical.

Measure the distance across the diameter of the circle created by the two pieces of tubing, from one flat surface to the other, and cut your wood, or pieces of wood, to this length. Lay the two pieces of wood next to each other, position the piano hinge on top and fasten it to the wood. This will allow it to fold in the center for easy storage.

Drill two holes into the flattened areas of each piece of tubing, eight holes all together. These holes will allow two wood screws to fasten each end of each piece of tubing, to the pieces of wood. When you put your tubing onto the wood, mount them just short of the inside edge of the wood. This will leave a gap between the ends of the tubing when they are in the finished stage. This gap between the tubes, is a necessary requirement to receive the TV signals.

Find the center point of balance and drill a hole for the 1/4" eye-bolt. Run the nut up high on the eye-bolt, then add the washer. Insert the eye-bolt through the hole you've drilled for this purpose, add the blind-nut on the end of the threaded portion of the eye-bolt now sticking through the wood, and tighten the nut down tight. This will pull the points on the blind-nut into the wood, locking it all in place. If you're going to use this antenna on a power vessel, consider using a 1.0" pipe flange under one side of the wood. This will allow the antenna to be mounted on a standard antenna mounting bracket.

An antenna coupler connector, (from Radio Shack) is now fastened to the antenna by securing one lead under a screw head on one side of the antenna, the other lead will go under a screw head on the other half of the antenna. With this in place, you have only to connect your television cable from the antenna to the television set.

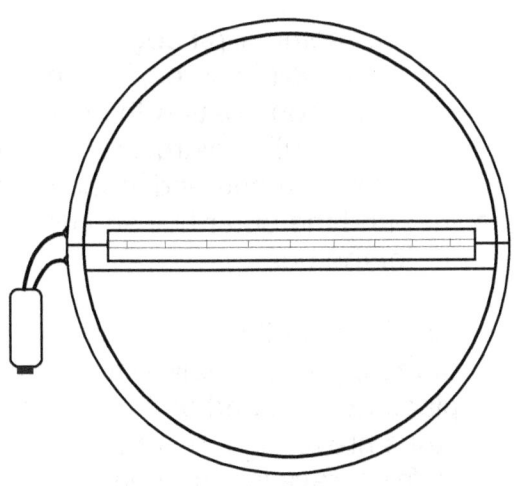

ENGINES

CURING ENGINE ROOM ODORS
While we were bringing our sailboat, "Itchy Feet,' home for the first time, Lyn mentioned that the engine was making the boat "smelly." This was a polite way of telling me that she did not want to be below deck when we were under power, and that I should see to the problem. Now this is a woman I've spent many a good year with on the water and off. As I have a mate who enjoys the waterways we travel, this is a relationship I mean to guard as long as possible.

Once we were in our home slip I began to look at the problem and the possible cures. This boat is not unlike other production boats with an inner liner and in this type of hull construction any smell in the boat can travel from one end to the other between the liner and the outer hull and ultimately enter the interior of the boat.

I found that I could isolate the engine compartment from the rest of the boat by installing two small bulkheads in place at each end of the engine's compartment, thus preventing the engine fumes and bilge odors from traveling throughout the boat.

After some careful measurements were taken, and the use of a saber saw, as well as a wood rasp, I had the panels made to fit the openings, but I did not want them to fit too tightly, so I left about a 1/4" clearance all around the edges.

In the piece of wood to be mounted at the aft end of the compartment, I cut a four-inch hole in the center. This hole would allow the mounting of a small 12 volt DC fan and a dryer duct hose to vent the fumes overboard. It is easiest to mount this fan and the metal vent collar onto the aft bulkhead before putting the bulkhead in place. As the forward panel did not need any holes in it, I was able to mount it without any extra effort. However, if there are any hoses, or electrical cables passing through this area in your boat, it is a simple matter of cutting a slot for their passage before putting the panel in place.

These small 12 volt DC fans can be purchased in electrical surplus stores as cooling fans. The sheet metal and flexible duct can be found in most hardware stores. I suggest wiring the fan using an inline fuse and a toggle switch wherever you decide to mount this part of the installation. I put mine right on my engine's instrument panel. These fans draw so little amperage that you can let them run for a length of time after you have shut the engine down. This really clears any heat or fumes out of the lower part of the boat. Should you want it to turn on, or off, when you are through with the engine, merely wire it through the ignition switch.

Originally I had decided to fiberglass these bulkheads in place, but used a can of expanding foam instead.

This helps cut down noise, and makes for an easier removal later, should it be desired. The foam actually locks the plywood bulkhead into place very well, and it sets up quickly.

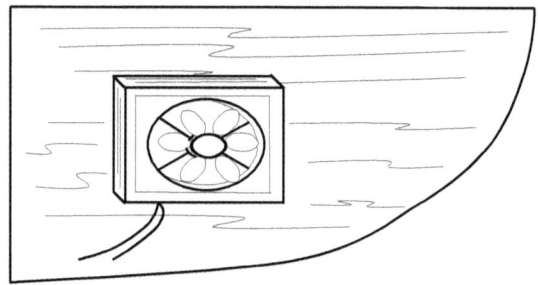

12 Volt Fan and wiring on forward side of panel

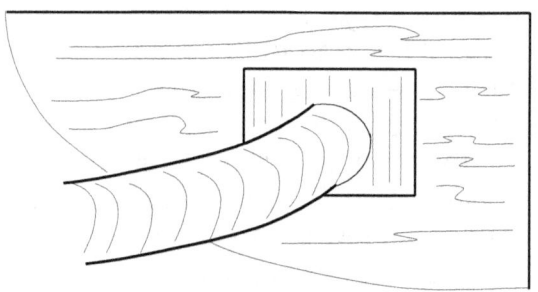

Dryer vent hose leading aft.

BILGES

BILGE ALARMS

A question that often nags at a boater is whether there is any water accumulating in the bilge. It could be water from the stuffing box on the propeller shaft, a rain water leak somewhere, a small persistent leak in a coolant line, perhaps one of your over board fittings, anyplace really.

In many cases in today's boats, there are carpets to be picked up, a table to be removed, maybe a cooler of some kind in the way, a sail bag, who knows what else, and you just don't want to move all of this stuff just to look in the bilge and find out it was for nothing.

To rid yourself of these nagging questions about water in your bilge, just build a simple bilge alarm. This is one of those projects that requires some patience and skill, but it can be built by anyone.

The parts list, and tools if necessary, are as follows, and can be purchased at any Radio Shack store.

    A small soldering iron, and solder
    Needle nose pliers
    Wire cutters
    Screw driver
    Solder less connector crimping tool
    Sharp knife
    RTV Sealant
    Oil resistant foam,(2.0" X 3.0" X .75")

One electronic circuit board - 276-147
One light emitting diode (LED) - 276-214
One 800 ohm resistor
Three toggle switches - 275-324

The components for the alarm unit will be soldered together on the circuit board according to the drawing. Drill holes to place the toggle switches on the board, and for the alarm Piezo module. 22 gauge wire is sufficient to connect all of the components together on the circuit board.

This alarm can be added to your existing bilge pump system, thus eliminating a new pump and pump switch. The wiring from your existing pump must be incorporated into this alarm system as well.

This system is built with the intention of allowing you to leave your bilge pump active without the alarm involved, or with the alarm in use.

Fasten the wiring from the Mercury switch to the bottom of the bilge area about two to three inches from the switch using RTV. If enough water seeps into your bilge it will raise this switch and the mercury will make contact inside and activate your alarm, depending on which switch setting you are using at the time.

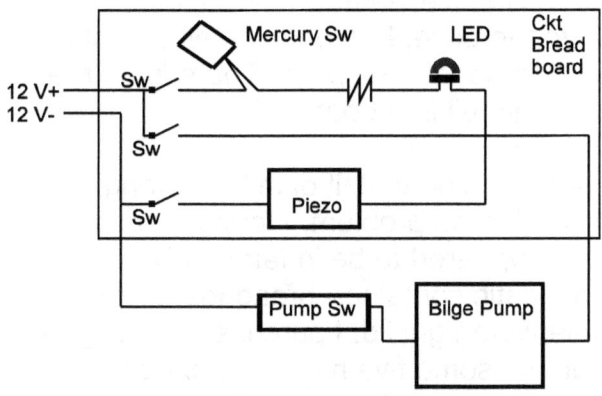

USING ICE MELT WATER

So you have an icebox on the boat, and where does the melted ice water go? Well, in most boats it goes into the bilge. I hate the smell of melted ice that has drained into the bilge. There is no reason to allow this smell in a boat.

Once I put my mind to it, it didn't take long to find a simple cure for the problem. I found a small foot pump that appeared to be in fair condition, and I bought a plastic container, bread-loaf size, with a removable watertight lid. I purchased a length of plastic tubing, some five minute epoxy and three plastic tubing fittings. Then a sink spigot from the local chandlery.

I epoxied one of the plastic fittings into the drain hole of our icebox, and after it set up, I pushed a length of plastic hose onto the fitting. This piece of tubing would reach the location in the bilge I had previously chosen for the plastic container.

Next I epoxied two fittings into the end of the food container, one at the bottom edge, and one well above the middle. The tubing from the icebox was pushed onto the upper fitting in the container.

I then mounted the foot pump in an out-of-the-way area in the galley. I ran a piece of tubing from the intake suction fitting on the pump, to the bottom fitting in the food container in the bilge.

From the other side of the pump, the outlet tubing was run up to the small spigot I installed in a hole I had drilled to one side of the galley's stainless steel sink.

This arrangement allows the water collected in the plastic container to be pumped into the sink, then it flows overboard through the sink drain. I make it a habit of pumping the water out each morning and evening, and the smell of melt water in my bilge is gone forever. In some cases this water can be used for rinsing dishes off before they are washed.

I didn't use hose clamps on any of these fittings, as this is not a water pressure situation. The fittings used are the type built for this purpose. Also, the size of the container you use for the water catchment would be restricted to the bilge space available in your particular situation.

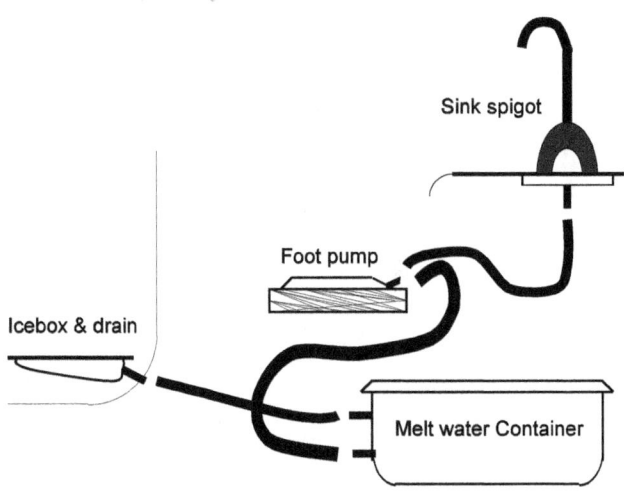

HOLDING TANKS

Often the size of the holding tanks provided in most production boats, are, or were, minimal. If you don't mind running up to the marina rest rooms as needed, you may get by on what you have. If not, I'd suggest you install larger holding tanks. These are not expensive, but more the problem of how to get them into the area you've chosen to install them. If you use your holding tanks exclusively, those trips to the pump out station in the winter can get, Uummm. . . .cold, and wet to say the least.

MAINTENANCE

DON'T HAUL IT OUT, CAREEN IT

There was a folding propeller on one of our first sailboats when we bought her. These are designed to reduce drag while under sail, and are fine if you race constantly. Not being racers, we have a laid back attitude such as raising our sails on Saturday and trimming them on Sunday.

However, I found this folding propeller didn't have sufficient bite in the water to back the boat down in reverse to my satisfaction, and this had to change because of the boating conditions under which we found ourselves.

The weather was cold enough to stop a local diver from going under the boat to change the propeller, and I didn't want to wait months to do the job. In addition, I didn't want to waste the money to haul the boat out just to change propellers.

The decision was made to careen the boat like they did in the old days. Before I committed myself to this maneuver, I contacted the builder to be sure I wouldn't put too much strain on the rigging. They assured me the boat could stand the strain, but they weren't sure I could pull her over far enough. On a Saturday morning we prepared to careen our boat over.

I went up the mast on the jib halyard to the spreaders, and tied the center of a three-quarter inch anchor line around the main mast. I left a small loop in the line, which was attached to the main halyard. This left two ends of the anchor line lying on deck. The mainsail halyard was raised to the masthead taking the line with it.

Utilizing a couple of empty double berthing slips, I tied our boat across the ends of the finger docks. The bow on one side, the stern on the other. The lines were left slack to allow for some freedom of hull movement during the process of being pulled over.

I used a piece of anchor chain looped around a main support beam on the main walkway, and bolted it together leaving about six inches of slack above the deck. A come-a-long hook was slipped around the chain and the hook moused closed so it would not slip off. The come-a-long cable was then pulled out to its full length.

The ends of the anchor lines going to the masthead were now on the main walkway with us, and with one of them our helpers, and there were several, hauled her down as far as she would come over by hand. While she was held over, the other line was cleated off to a large cleat on the walkway. Once cleated off, the other line was taken to the end of the cable from the come-a-long and a bowline knot was now tied into the anchor line at that spot.

With the loop formed by the bowline slipped over the hook on this end of the come-a-long cable, we cranked in the slack as far as we could. The other line we had started with was now cleated off again, and the come-a-long cable released and pulled back out again. A new bowline knot was tied in the anchor line, again slipped onto the hook, and the process repeated until the boat was hauled over far enough to change the propeller. With a new propeller, a large adjustable wrench, a pair of long nose pliers and an assortment of cotter pins, the change was made from our dinghy off the boat's stern.

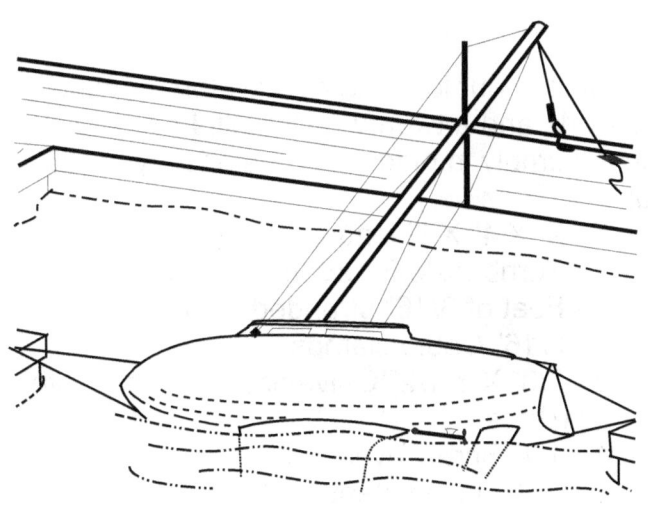

DINGHY STORAGE

I made the mistake, a couple of winters back, of leaving my dinghy on my foredeck and the winter winds put it back into the water when I wasn't around to help. The damage was minimal, but could have been disastrous. This then, presented the problem of where to keep it during the times it wasn't being used, but handy when it was needed.

I considered leaving it in the water between our boat, and our neighbors, but soon found there just wasn't enough room, so I contacted our marina office and got permission to build a support for my dink at the head of our slip. This keeps the dinghy out of the water to avoid bottom growth and damage.

After a visit to our local hardware store, a couple of hours work, and a twenty-dollar bill, I had the whole assembly in place. For materials you will need:

- 1 - 2" X 4" X 8' long
- 1 - Turnbuckle for supporting the dinghy
- 6 - Feet of 3/16" stranded cable
- 4 - 3/16" Cable clamps
- 2 - 3/8" X 3-1/2" Galvanized lag bolts with washers
- 4 - 1/4" Screw eyes
- 1 - Galvanized cleat
- 2 - 'L' Screws for supporting the bottom of the dinghy
- 3 - 1/2" #8 galvanized wood screws for fastening the two by four to the dock.

1 - Sheet metal end cap for the top of the two by four, for protection.

2 - Cable clamps to fit the size of the wire cable.
A length of line, to be determined by you, to tie the dinghy in place. I also used a hand saw, drill motor, and an adjustable wrench.

You'll need to cut two pieces of wood 8.0" long, from your 8' 2" X 4" these are to be used for the bottom dinghy supports located on the side of the dock edge.

Fasten the upright support to the dock using two galvanized lag bolts and washers.

At the bottom of the support install one of the screw eyes. A line will run from the eye screw, around the dinghy, through the upper eye screw and down to the cleat mounted on the back of the upright support. This line secures the dinghy in place.

Place an eye screw on the back side of the upright support, 6.0" from the top. This is for the cable attachment. Drill pilot holes for all of the fasteners to prevent splitting the wood.

Place a metal cap on the 2" X 4" to protect it from the abuse of the cable and line leading over the top.

Decide where the bottom of the dinghy will rest against the dock, and screw the two short pieces of 2" X 4" to the dock with wood screws.

Screw one of the 'L' shaped screws into the center of each one of the bottom supports. These 'L' screws will support the bottom of the dinghy and lock it into place.

Open the eye on one end of the turnbuckle and slip it into one of the eye screws. Then close it again locking the eye screw to the bottom of the turnbuckle.

Run a line from this eye screw, out and around the dinghy, up through the eye screw at the top of the support, over the top of the upright, and down to the cleat on the dock.

Insert one end of the wire cable through the unused eye of the turnbuckle, forming a loop and using one of the clamps to close the loop, locking it closed. Run the wire cable up through the screw eye on top of the upright support, and form another loop to be closed and locked with the other cable clamp.

Now you can adjust the tension in the wire cable with the turnbuckle until the slack is taken up, putting some tension on the upright support.

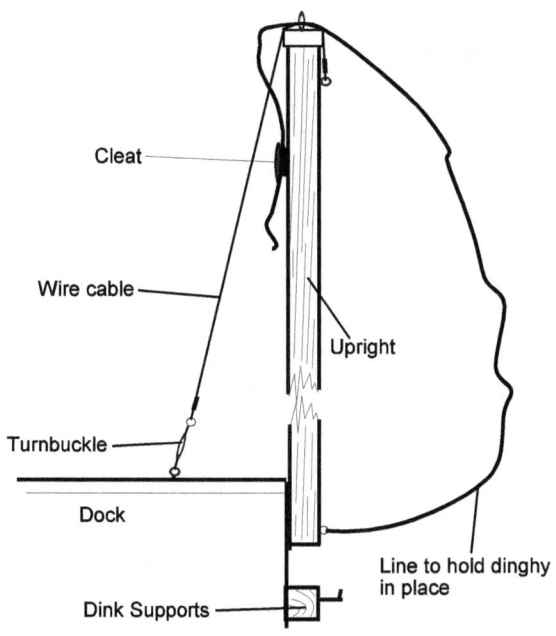

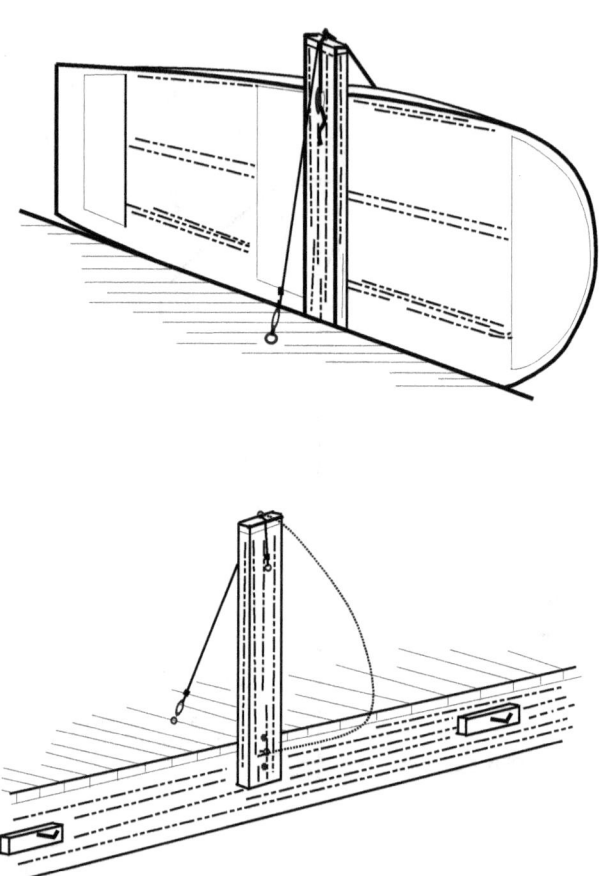

GETTING HIGH

I'm on my way to the top of the mast, again, my knees are locking against the cold metal, my fingers are glued to anything I touch. This time it's to straighten a seagull damaged wind indicator, and I hate going up there. Anyone who has been at the top of a sailboat mast knows this fear. It matters not how high the mast is because if you fall the stop is the same.

Most often there is concern about who is on the deck and in control of your ascent and decent. I finally decided it was time to be in control of my own coming and going when I had to go up there, and depending on my own abilities.

I attached a three-fall block, three pulleys in one with a thimble fitting on each end of the block, to the main halyard. A half inch line is attached to the bottom of one block, then the other end is threaded through each fall of both blocks. That end, after being threaded through all of the falls, is loose and at deck level, and you should tie a figure eight knot in the end to prevent its getting away from you and whipping through each fall unchecked. The Bosun's chair is attached to the thimble portion of the bottom block.

The ratio for a pair of three fall blocks is seven to one. This means that if you weigh 140 pounds, it will be equivalent to pulling 20 pounds up the mast. After hauling the upper block to your masthead, cleat the main halyard off securely.

Step into your Bosun's chair and attach the safety line from the chair around the mast. The hard part is in pulling the entire length of line to get you to the masthead. With a fifty foot mast, and a three fall block, you will be pulling 350 feet of line. Attaching a small weight to the end of this line, and the line placed in a bucket, will insure the line going into the bucket as well and out of the way without snagging on something.

When you get to the height you want to work at, use the line you have been using to tie a knot through the eye fitting at the top of your Bosun's chair. When you get ready to go back down, you'll have to pull yourself up a bit to release the knot.

One final matter, storing the rig without its becoming tangled, can be avoided by two or three loops of the line, then chain stitching the rest of it around the loops. It can be stored in the bucket until the next time you need to go to the top again.

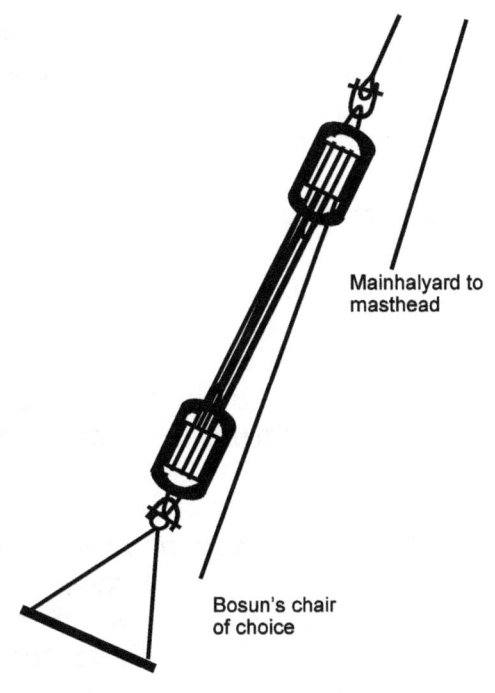

SIMPLIFIED MOORING

I stopped to visit with some hew boating neighbors at their boathouse, and while there, I happened to see one of the neatest boat mooring gadgets I've ever come across. When their boating day is over, they drive their boat into the boathouse well, stop and merely reach up for their mooring lines. That's right, reach up for them.

Their mooring lines go up, through a single fall block, then out to the outside wall and another single fall block, then down to a metal loop fixed in concrete which is inside an eighteen-inch piece of three-inch PVC pipe. The three-inch PVC pipe slides up and down inside a four-inch piece of PVC pipe. The four inch piece is fastened to the outside wall.

Each mooring line, two forward and two aft, has an eye spliced into the end. When the mooring line is pulled down and the loop slipped over the boat's cleat, it lifts the weighted piece of three inch PVC pipe inside the four-inch piece, and the weight keeps the boat centered in the slip and reduces impact strain on the boat's cleats during wind and wakes from passing boats.

When they leave the slip, the lines are released from the cleats, and the weights pull them up and out of the way. I would not attempt this project on a boat larger than twenty-five feet as the weight needed to hold the boat in place might be excessive.

It's a simple project to build with a minimum of tools. You'll need a hacksaw, a large screwdriver, an electric drill and a hammer.

Materials for four mooring lines.
> 4-pieces of 4.0" PVC pipe five-feet long, this length may be influenced by other factors.
> 4-pieces of 3.0" PVC pipe
> 4-4.0" PVC pipe caps
> 4-pieces of ½" threaded rod, or something similar

You could use a long eye-bolt with a nut on the end to act as an anchor in the concrete.
> You could also use a long piece of building reinforcing steel rod bent into a long 'U' shape.
> 4-1/2" nuts and washers
> 8-pulleys for the size of mooring line you'll be using.
> 12-stainless steel pipe clamps for the 4.0" PVC
> 1-Small can of PVC pipe cement
> Fasteners to install the straps and pulleys to the building.
> Bags of pre-mix concrete to fill the pieces of 3.0" PVC.

Which ever method you choose, the threaded rod or eye-bolt, etc. put a nut and washer about one inch up from the bottom, and begin filling the 3.0" pipe full of concrete, keeping the threaded rod or whatever centered as you do so. The preference would be to have this holding device as deep into the concrete as possible.

While you are pouring the concrete inside the pipe, you may want to tamp it down, or to tap on the outside of the pipe with a hammer, or whatever, to work out any bubbles which will help prevent voids.

While your concrete sets up, glue the pipe caps onto one end of the 4.0" PVC pipes. You may want to consider drilling a small drain hole into the pipe cap as well. Then fasten these to the outside wall framing, capped end down, with pipe straps using heavy screws or lag bolts. You may not need to locate the pipes in exact alignment with your mooring cleats on the boat.

Fasten the pulleys to the overhead beams. Bolt one pulley over each deck cleat, and one pulley over each piece of 4.0" PVC pipe.

Put your eye splice into the end of each mooring line, then thread the lines up through the overhead pulley, then out to the one near the wall, and down to its respective weight, and slide the weight into the 4.0" PVC pipe guide. When the mooring lines are attached to the boat, you should have about a foot of the weight still inside the guide pipe.

A few precautions: the cleats must be through bolted with backer plates. The pulleys must be securely fastened. The weights should be adjusted for the boat; lighter boats-less weight, heavier boats more weight. Use good line, heavy fasteners, and stout pulleys. Above all, this is not a job to save money. This is a project to keep your boat safe at any cost.

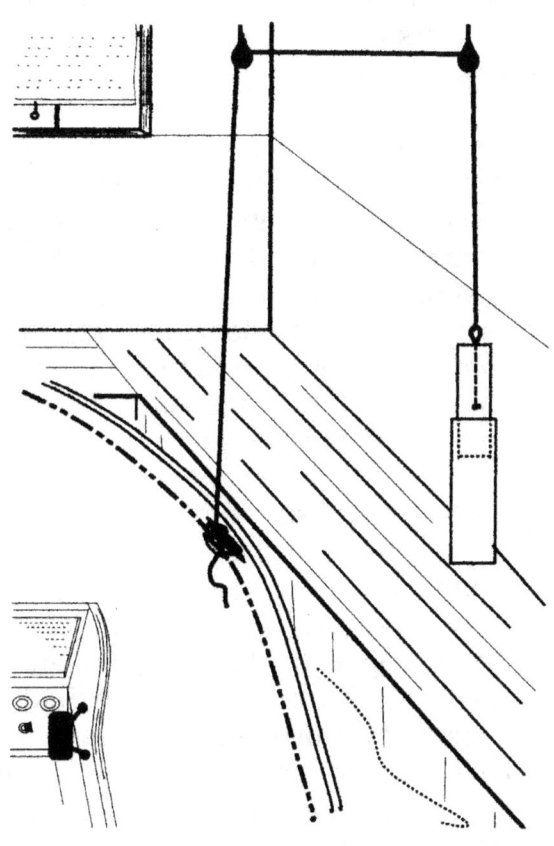

STRUT BEARING PRESS

On a recent haul-out, one of the yard's personnel destroyed a new strut bearing as he heated the strut while trying to get the bearing to fit. His use of a torch burned the rubber beyond use. I've also watched people try to beat strut bearings into place, usually without success. Yet, there is a method that works most of the time once you have the propeller shaft removed.

Generally the bearing is held in place with set screws, which must be loosened. Remove the blade from your hacksaw, turn it over and push it through the strut bearing and re-attach it to the frame. Take your time, but make two cuts through the bearings outer brass cylinder. This will relieve the pressure on the bearing, and the remnants should now be tapped out of the strut. Using a brass bar and hammer works best.

To build your own strut bearing press, purchase a piece of iron pipe that is slightly larger in diameter, and longer than the bearing you are replacing. You will also need a threaded rod 5/8" in diameter, and at least twice as long as the bearing plus a few inches, three nuts to fit the threaded rod, and six heavy washers that will overlap the outside diameter of the bearing. You will also need some heavy washers that are the same size as the outside diameter of the bearing. These washers must fit inside the diameter of the pipe so that they can be pulled through at the same time you pull the bearing through.

To remove the bearing, you begin by threading two of the nuts onto one end of the threaded rod a short distance from one end. Using two wrenches, tighten the two nuts together by turning the wrenches toward each other. This will lock the nuts onto the threaded rod so they will not move.

Slip the smaller washers onto the threaded rod and push the rod through the bearing, the pipe and the larger washers. Now thread the remaining nut onto the other end of the rod until it runs up against the washers.

Check the other end to be certain the washers will ride on the edges of the bearing, but will not hang up on the edge of the strut as the bearing is being pulled out.

The inside edge of the pipe must be outside the edge of the strut bearing. When the single nut is tightened, it will pull the bearing out of the strut and into the pipe. You may have to hold the doubled nuts with a wrench while you tighten the single nut.

To pull the new bearing into place, slip the bearing over the threaded rod until it meets the smaller washers.

The threaded rod is pushed through the strut, and the large washers are placed over the rod and then run the remaining nut up against them.

The process of tightening the single nut will pull the new bearing into place in the strut.

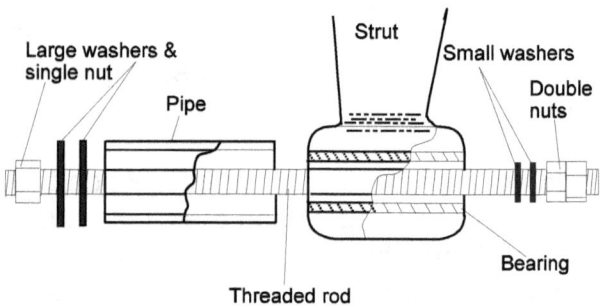

NAVIGATION

HOME MADE SPEED LOGS

We were on a summer cruise that started in May, and our knotmeter stopped working. Granted this is not a piece of gear that is absolutely necessary, but it is nice to have working when you have one. Mine wasn't.

I tried every trick I could think of to get it going again, but to no avail. I tried running a line under the boat to break it free, I tried powering the boat in reverse as fast as I could, but zip, nada, nothing. It seemed okay on the last haul out or I would have just replaced the unit.

Now, however, I wanted a speed log that worked, and I had one to use sitting in the refrigerator. I explained my plight to my sweety and she decided to use the last of the milk making goodies for later. A milk jug is a good speed log with a piece of light line tied to it's handle, and with the cap intact. A fifty foot, plus a few feet, nylon line with a bowline works very well. You'll need enough line to drop a loop over a cleat, or winch when in use so that you don't lose it to the elements. And, when you're through with it, it can be stored in a locker until your chip log, as they were called in the past, is needed again.

When you have your chip log assembled, you put the loop over a cleat, then drop the plastic milk bottle into the water and count off the seconds until it reaches the end of its tether. You know, you count, one thousand one, one thousand two, one thousand three, etc.

You may have to experiment with the line as it pays out. You don't want to have to haul it back in several times to get a proper count of elapsed seconds. You might try letting the loops of line fall off your hand as it pays out, or loops laid out in such a manner where the line can just move easily from some location on your stern deck. If the line tangles, you won't get a proper count on the seconds.

Now for the easy part, once you have counted the seconds it took for the milk bottle to reach the end of its line, you can compare those seconds with the speed chart below.

The formula for this table is: You divide fifty feet of line by the seconds, then multiply that times 3600. This is the amount of seconds in an hour. Then divide that sum into the feet of a nautical mile, or 6080'. This will give you your boat's speed through the water. As an example:

 50 divided by 9 Sec. X 3600 divided by 6080 = 3.289 knots

Feet	Seconds	Knots	Feet	Seconds	Knots
50	1	29.6	50	15	1.9
	2	14.8		16	1.8
	3	9.8		17	1.7
	4	7.4		18	1.6
	5	5.9		19	1.5
	6	4.9		20	1.4
	7	4.2		21	1.4
	8	3.7		22	1.3
	9	3.2		23	1.2
	10	2.9		24	1.2
	11	2.6		25	1.1
	12	2.4		26	1.1
	13	2.2		27	1.0
	14	2.1		28	0.98

CELESTIAL NAVIGATION, ANYPLACE

My celestial navigation skills go right out the portal if I can't practice them occasionally, and a false horizon mirror never quite helped me. Either I couldn't find a decent location to put the mirror, or the sun would shine off the mirror, blinding me in the process.

On a recent day out sailing, I happened to look over the stern of the boat to the southern horizon. Lo and behold, I realized I actually had a horizon and immediately thought of the needed practice with the sextant. That night as I lay in the vee berth, it dawned on me that I could practice my celestial navigation any time I choose.

This is how you go about doing this yourself. The next time you are out on the boat where you can see the horizon, sit down in your cockpit and look aft toward the horizon over, or under, your stern rail. When you find where it is located on a stern pushpit stanchion, wrap a piece of black electrical tape around the upright portion at that spot. Do this on both sides, or at any location you might use for a shot.

A note here, the horizon is not as far away as you may think. According to Dutton's Navigation and Piloting tables, if your eye height is five feet above the water, the horizon is two and six-tenths miles away.

Don't allow anyone to help you mark your stanchions, as any weight transfer will alter your final readings.

One problem you may encounter is the boat swinging at anchor. Be patient. After the boat settles at the end of a swing, then you can bring the sun's lower limb down to the black electrical tape on the most convenient stanchion. After each sun shot note the time and write it down along with the sextant altitude. Take several shots so you can abandon the questionable ones later.

Time is another important factor that is often overlooked. Be certain your watch is set correctly. I have a small radio that provides the Greenwich time ticks, and this allows me the correct time with which to set my watch or clocks. If you use an Almanac and the associated tables, work up the shots. If you are using a celestial calculator, remember to add your current time zone as well. The first time I tried this method, I forgot to add this factor in, and my LOPs came out three thousand miles from my DR position.

Using this method of practice for your celestial navigation will make it much easier to find your location the next time you are doing it for the real thing. You can produce the same results with start shots by adding reflective tape to the stanchions, but you might have to provide some reflecting light so you can see the tape.

One problem you may encounter is the boat swinging at anchor. Be patient. After the boat settles at the end of a swing, then you can bring the sun's lower limb down to the black electrical tape on the most convenient stanchion. After each sun shot note the time and write it down along with the sextant altitude. Take several shots so you can abandon the questionable ones later.

Time is another important factor that is often overlooked. Be certain your watch is set correctly. I have a small radio that provides the Greenwich time ticks, and this allows me the correct time with which to set my watch or clocks. If you use an Almanac and the associated tables, work up the shots. If you are using a celestial calculator, remember to add your current time zone as well. The first time I tried this method, I forgot to add this factor in, and my LOPs came out three thousand miles from my DR position.

Using this method of practice for your celestial navigation will make it much easier to find your location the next time you are doing it for the real thing.

You can produce the same results with start shots by adding reflective tape to the stanchions, but you might have to provide some reflecting light so you can see the tape.

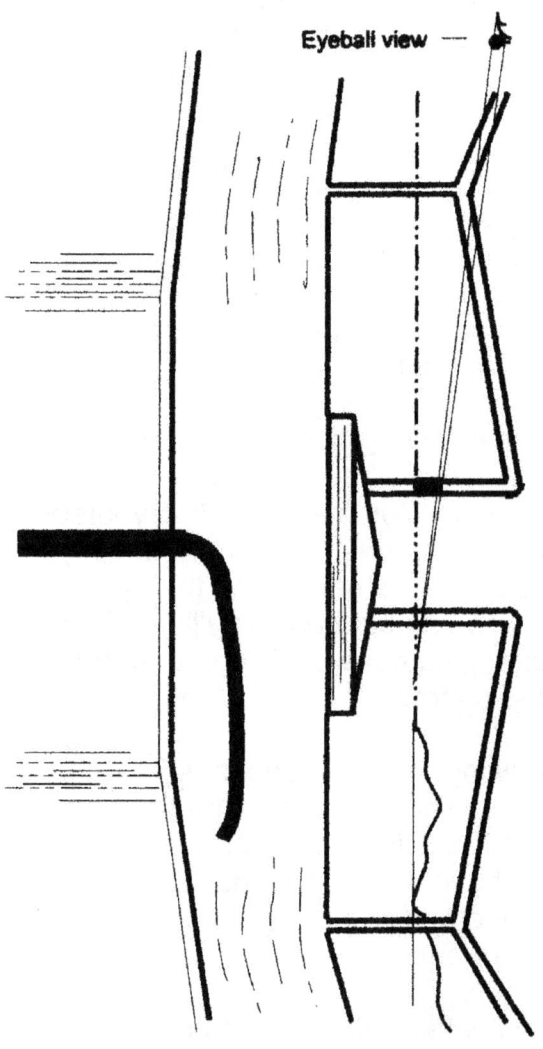

MAKING PERSONAL CHARTS

In our years of gunkholing, we've found many out of the way coves to spend a few quiet days at anchor. The problem most often encountered is that charts of the area rarely list any detail of these locations.

If it's a spot I am unable to visit often, I tend to forget a few details between visits. Consequently I've made it a habit to keep a notebook of my homemade charts on board. Then, as needed, I can quickly refer to my own charts for entry, or the best place to anchor, and why.

You, too, can make your own charts of your favorite locations when none exist, and you can do so quite simply. You may even find yourself enjoying this kind of entertainment while you are in the area. The items need to do this you most likely already have on your boat. You'll need a dinghy, a hand bearing compass, a 360 degree protractor, pencil and paper.

Start by taking compass bearings from the cockpit of your boat. These will be to the prominent landmarks in the immediate area around the boat. Once you have these bearings, put a dot or a mark of some kind and mark it with an 'A', in the center of a piece of paper.

Place the center of the protractor over this dot. At the protractors edge, mark the compass bearing marks and run lines from the point out over each dot, and to the edge of your paper. Label each line with its appropriate compass bearing and name; that is rock, sandbar, etc. Use the drawings as a guide.

With this done, go ashore to one of your chosen locations. From this location take compass bearings to all of the other points you've selected. On your chart drawing, this will be labeled as 'B'. You can do this from as many of your locations as you choose.

Back on board the boat, and using your protractor over position 'B', add these new lines to your chart drawing. When these lines are drawn, the magic starts to unfold. Freehand the surrounding shoreline onto your drawing and use the label names of the items you've selected, such as rock, sandbar. . .. using the intersecting points from the positions you used, 'A' and 'B'.

After erasing your compass bearing lines you can add the final details to your chart. You may consider using a lead line (or a heavy nut or bolt tied to a piece of line) to measure the water depth at low tide, if this is a condition in your area, noting the depths on your chart. With this done, the next time you're in the area you'll have a nice chart handy.

The degrees used on these charts are for descriptive purposes only.

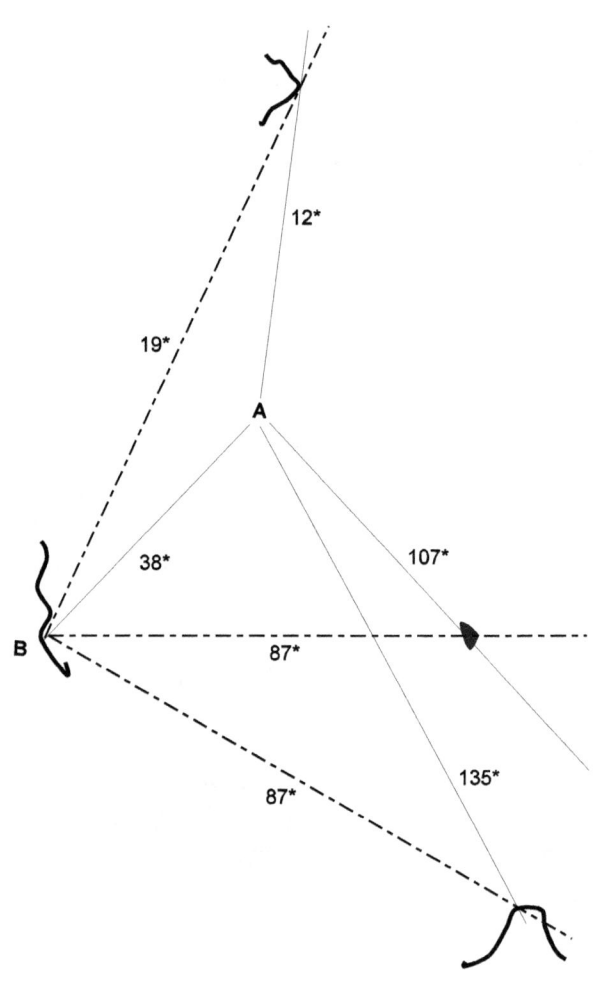

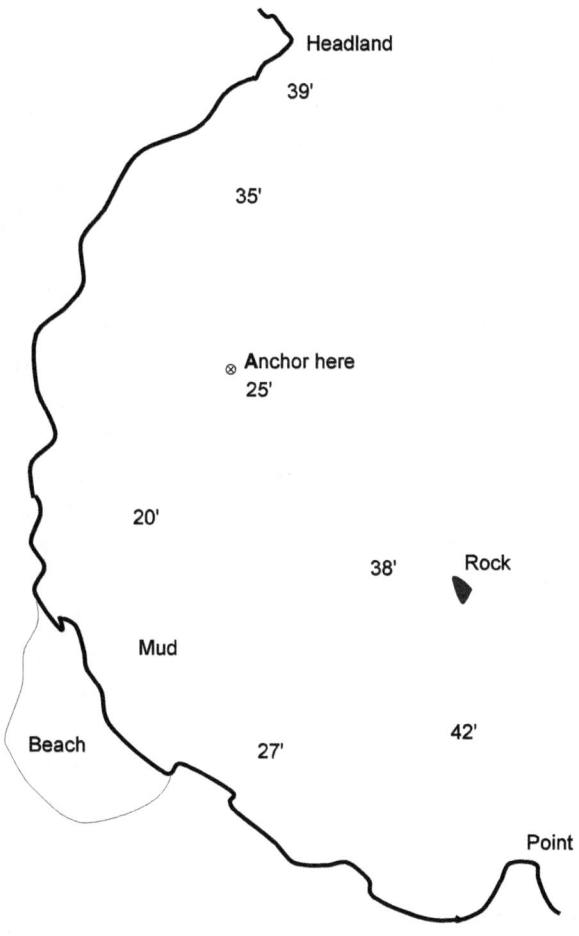

USEFUL INFORMATION

AFRAID TO ANCHOR?
Should you happen to ask boaters this question, the answer you're likely to hear is, "Heck no." "Of course not." In reality they lack confidence in their anchoring technique. If you are the type who goes from dock to dock and never anchors, you are really missing out on some wonderful experiences, and one of the more satisfying aspects of boating.

The lack of confidence, especially with new boaters, comes from many sources, one of those sources is the stories we as boaters like to tell as we visit with other boaters. These are not the stories about the great times, the wonderful sunsets, the quiet of an area, the ultimate privacy, and that sort of stuff. No, these are the horror stories about boats, other than our own, such as dragging anchors in the middle of a storm. In the eyes of new boaters, in their minds-eye they see their boats being crushed on rocks, stuck with the loss of all hands. No wonder they don't anchor.

There are some anchoring basics we can discuss that should help you gain confidence. Actually the only way to gain the knowledge and the confidence, is to go out and anchor. Even if it is only for the day.

Pick up a chart of the area you wish to visit, and on that chart you will see an indication of what kind of bottom conditions exist in the area. These are often noted as 'S' for sandy, 'M' for mud, 'Rky' for rocky, etc. While at the chandlery, ask the clerk for a booklet that has a pictorial explanation of all the symbols on the charts.

Choose a spot to put your hook down that will offer you good holding, such as mud or sand, and be sure that you have ample water at low tide, if you're in a tidal situation. Check for underwater obstructions such as rocks, sunken pilings, shipwrecks, cable crossings, and the like.

 These are some of the items that will determine how much anchor line you have out, but there are other factors to consider in the anchorage area you choose. One of those will be mother nature. Should it become necessary, can you escape the area if need be? Will you be anchoring in an area where the prevailing winds, or currents, offer a lee shore should you drag the hook? Will the currents increase due to tidal flow. Small headlands, can offer nice places to hide behind when there are currents, or winds. Always choose the location carefully.

Scope is a measurement for the amount of anchor line used. Some boaters say a three-to-one scope is good for day anchoring. That is, three feet of anchor line in the water for each foot of water depth under the boat. However, after spending fifteen years of traveling on boats, my preference is five-to-one. In heavy weather even more line may be needed. If you start out with at least five-to-one, it may save you a trip topside in the middle of the night when the winds increase.

The type of anchor you choose is one of a personal choice. My first experience at anchoring was with a Danforth anchor in an area where a lot of kelp was present. I, being inexperienced, did not know that to attempt to put a Danforth down in this kind of bottom was like greasing the anchor because it just slides across the bottom.

Many boaters use Danforth anchors continually. In my case I keep one as a spare, but my anchor of choice is the Plow type. I have found it will dig in quickly, and it will stay there in nearly any condition. The Bruce anchor is gaining in popularity and requires less scope, yet has good holding power.

When you arrive in your chosen area, motor through it to find a water depth of your choosing, and look for any surprises that may be lurking nearby. Once the area is decided upon, motor to it, even drifting into it, drop your anchor, then pay out your anchor line until your hook is resting on the bottom.

Once the anchor is down, you can back the boat down to set the hook, then pay out the remaining line you intend to use and cleat the line off securely. When you are backing the boat down under power, you may notice the boat will dip slightly as the hood digs in solid. In popular anchorages, it is not uncommon to run a stern line to the beach to keep from swinging on the hook in tight quarters.

Once you are anchored it is a good practice to take a fix on things around you, even using a hand bearing compass if you like. This will allow you to monitor your position on occasion to see if you are still in the same place. In tidal areas, you will notice some change as the depth of the water increases, or decreases. Most good anchors will reset if pulled loose, and often deeper than before.

It is a common fact that after you have spent some time anchored in the same spot, that the hook may be buried so deep that it can be difficult to pull out. In this case you can pull all of the slack line aboard and cleat the line off.

Back at the helm, power over the anchor. Keep in mind propeller's love anchor lines. Generally you only have to get the boat moving, then take the engine out of gear to let the boat drift. Move to the foredeck, and again pull in as much slack as you can, and cleat it off. You can repeat this procedure until you have pulled the hook free from the bottom. When it is free, bring it up quickly, but safely. I recommend using a bucket of water to wash down the deck area after the anchor has been stowed.

If you don't have a windlass, but have the hook snagged, pull the line as tight as possible, cleat if off, then move aft to rock the boat's bow up and down. Go forward and repeat the process until the anchor comes free. If this doesn't do the trick, keep the line taut, and wait for the tide to lift the boat, and hopefully pull your hook out.

Should you ever find your anchor is raising some kind of debris, tie a temporary line around the debris, drop your anchor slightly to get it clear of the foul material, then release the debris from your temporary line.

If the wind picks up while you are anchored, check how much swinging room you have available. If you started with a five-to-one scope you may be okay. If it really starts to blow, let out more scope. Seven-to-one should hold you in most conditions, but a ten-to-one is better.

This is a choice you must make at the time. I recommend you have at least 300 feet of anchor line aboard, plus ample chain between the anchor rode and the anchor.

If you use all chain rode, use a ten foot length of nylon line, or longer if needed, as a snubber line. This line will attach to your anchor chain, preferably with a hook on one end, the other end going to a good sound cleat. Fasten the snubber hook to the chain a distance out from the boat and cleat the other end off to the chosen cleat. Before you cleat it off, pull it in slightly to create a small loop of chain hanging loosely between the boat and the snubber's hook.

If you get into the anchorage first, you set the anchoring precedent for all others that follow as they become the burdened vessels. If, after anchoring, they swing too close, they should move. If they show no response to the danger, you might bring it to their attention, or make the change on your own.

Beware of the skipper who stands on the bow, lowers the anchor straight down until it touches the bottom, throws out a loop or two of line, cleats it off and goes aft. The boat won't stay anchored long, and if he is upwind of you he becomes even more dangerous to you.

If there are two of you aboard and one stays at the helm while the other does the anchor work, using hand signals will eliminate the need for shouting instructions to one another. These signals can be anything, just work them out before you start the procedure.

Once you have spent time at anchor in private splendor, it will become difficult to spend time at a dock.

ANIMALS ON BOARD

When I moved aboard my first sailboat, I had a Dachshund that thought he owned me, and of course he did. Before I moved aboard I had not taken into account the extra needs of a pet owner under this kind of living condition. It wasn't long when I began to think, 'Is it worth it?' This is a question each of us as pet owners who live aboard have to consider, but I did enjoy Fritz's company on the boat.

However, before you, yourself, undertake the keeping of a pet on board, there are a number of items you should consider first. Part of this is the kind of animal you want as a pet around the boat.

Some animals do better aboard a boat than others. For instance, the better dogs to consider keeping on a boat are: Dachshunds, Beagles, most Poodles, Spaniels and of course, Retrievers. These are water world dogs and they take to it naturally.

If you have an older dog there may be a problem for it to alter its lifestyle to this kind of living, and if it doesn't like the water, don't force the issue. The short haired breeds usually do better than those with long hair. If you are presently living aboard and want to get a dog, you should get them as puppies, as they stand a better chance to acclimate themselves to this environment.

Plus, when the animal learns from their youth to accept your lifting them in and out of a dinghy, you will rarely receive many scratches on the arms from their resistence of being lifted.

Cats often fit this lifestyle much better than dogs, and most boaters have less trouble caring for a cat aboard, also they are more practical than dogs. They rarely need trips ashore, and a kitty litter pan works well for both of you. Especially when it comes to rowing ashore in a heavy rainstorm just so the dog can take care of it's business.

Lyn and I tried moving one of our older cats on board our sailboat and the cat did okay as long as the engine wasn't running. When we had to run our engine, some kind of noise seemed to bother his hearing and he began to yowl loudly, and would continue to do so as long as the engine was running. When we turned the engine off, it was like turning a switch off on the cat as well. We forgot trying to move that cat on board, and he found a home with one of our relatives.

A cat will rarely run off to chase some unknown foe waiting in the brush as a dog might, but a cat will roam around the marina. If you have a neighbor who complains about your cat spending time on his/her boat you will have to address this situation.

Dogs need plenty of exercise and they rarely get it on a small boat deck. They have to be able to go ashore to run and play, and they should have this ability three of four times a day. One of these shore time periods should be for an hour duration. The evening is often the best, right after they have eaten. This will facilitate their need for regularity and help them adjust to a schedule that you can set.

There are issues in taking care of an animal that seem natural to most owners, yet I see them being ignored frequently.

Such as letting your dog swim in saltwater or a polluted stream. In most cases this is okay, but if left without a freshwater rinse, it can cause skin problems for the dog. If you live in a saltwater environment, most dogs know instinctively not to drink too much saltwater, but on occasion one will overdo this seemingly simple act and become sick. This will happen, of course, when you are back on board and the dog is on the carpet of your main cabin sole.

In caring for a dog that has had too much saltwater to drink, give him/her a small amount of Pepto-Bismol and do not feed the dog for awhile. Of course if you keep fresh water available and renew it several times a day, odds are your dog won't drink the saltwater.

On the subject of water, do not provide ice water for a dog that is overheated; let the dog cool off normally. Ice water can cause diarrhea for a dog, and this is not going to make you happy.

Keeping food aboard for a pet should not normally be a problem. But dried foods can attract moisture so they need to be kept in a waterproof container. Canned foods work very well for both you and your pet.

Another good item to consider, is your dog's way of thinking. Dogs are very possessive of their homes and surroundings. With this in mind, keep your dog below deck when you're coming into a dock, especially if it is one not known to the dog. If left to roam the deck, one of those neighborly types who offer to take a dock line, could find a dog's teeth embedded in their hand when reaching to stop your movement by taking hold of your gunwale or toe rail.

Another hazard with a pet being topside when maneuvering into a dock or mooring, is their innate ability to be underfoot just when you least need them to be in the way.

With a cat aboard, it is a good idea to keep a piece of carpeting rigged on the stern and down to the water so that the cat can climb back aboard. Cats are good swimmers, but they may not be able to swim long distance like many dogs can. I know of a charter captain whose cat climbed up his anchor rode one time after falling overboard while in port.

When you keep pets aboard there are a few things to consider when you invite friends aboard. As guests, men friends will deal with animals aboard your boat better than women. The reason for this is because men in general are more untidy than women.

When a woman sits down on your settee, then stands up to leave and finds her skirt is covered with cat or dog hair, she will not be happy. She may also never come aboard again. Men on the other hand will simply attempt to brush the offending hairs from their pants, though they may not sit down if they come back for another visit.

When you live aboard with pets you may become un-aware of the smells a boat accumulates from pets. It is the wise pet owner who airs the boat regularly, and this doesn't mean once a month. This will need to be done very often, if not daily, and an air freshener may be needed. To enter a boat that has several animals aboard, and that has not been aired out, is not to be entered again for most visitors.

Birds, though many owners find them to be good pets, can be very messy. Especially if it is the kind of bird who has freedom to fly around inside the boat's interior. I've been on a boat whose owner kept a Cockatoo, and in going below I found the main salon table covered with paper which was covered with Cockatoo droppings and a perch for the bird to sit on while loose inside the boat.

And, can you imagine getting up during the night to go to the head and walking in your bare feet across a cabin sole covered in cracked or loose birdseed. Yes, you have the correct picture of this event. There are only a few who do this more than once.

LIVING ABOARD

While Lyn and I lived aboard our boats over the years, truly wonderful years, we often met others who were considering moving aboard their own boats. As we would chat amongst ourselves, they would always ask questions about this lifestyle. One of those would be, "What is the best time to move aboard?"

My usual answer would be more of an explanation than an answer such as, "I'm not sure there is a best time." As it happens, If you move aboard just as winter is approaching, you encounter the full impact of cramped quarters with all kinds of personal gear and clothing still in the way; all this while the winter elements wait for you just a few feet away. During your first winter aboard, in the cold, often accompanied by dampness, and even ice, can provide a disheartening feeling among those who do not know what to expect of this lifestyle.

Then of course, when spring arrives, the morning sun warms you as you sit out in the cockpit, and the world looks good. If you move aboard in the summertime, you still have to find someplace to put all of the items you've brought with you. All the stuff you thought you couldn't live without, you now find you can.

No matter when you move aboard, you'll find some things you used at home, that is, in a house, are not going to work in this environment. The hard part is getting through your first winter in comfort. After that all the rest is a piece of cake. Well, mostly.

Living on board a boat is not a lifestyle that can be easily explained. If you are of the mind to live aboard, you will enjoy it. If you are moving aboard, but don't really want to, you will find every excuse to dislike it. Of course there are drawbacks, but every lifestyle has its own drawbacks.

Another question that arises is, "What is the best boat length to live aboard?" The answer is, "The one you can afford without sucking your bank account dry." This means you have to consider boat payments, if you're like most of us, the cost of moorage, insurance, etc. We've met couples living aboard twenty-four footers, one couple raising two children on a twenty seven footer, and a couple living on a forty eight footer, who didn't understand how anyone could live on any thing smaller.

Many who consider this lifestyle are concerned about the money they think they will save, because they will no longer have a home to pay for and to maintain. There are costs for living aboard that you will encounter. Most marinas have live aboard restrictions in place, often imposed by the county in which the marina resides. The general rule, but not always the case, is that they can have ten percent of their boat slips allotted to live aboards.

Also live aboards pay a higher moorage rate. The additional costs for live-aboards cover their electrical power and in some cases, the additional garbage, and the extra water usage, plus other related costs.

There are strict regulations as to sewage, and personal behavior, but marina managers also know that your presence, as a live aboard, cuts down on theft in the marina, as well. Most often the marina managers will try to keep some space between their live aboards. They do this by having a few boats between you and others living aboard. This allows more personal privacy for both parties.

Your boating insurance may also change. I'm not sure why, but it seems insurance companies think a boat is safer if you don't live aboard. Ignorance on their part means more money out of your pocket. Their reasoning may be based on the amount of boats using propane stoves, or propane heaters, as well as gasoline engines.

Anyone who has a vessel with these conditions should already be well aware that these are indeed dangers and take evasive action by installing gasoline, or propane sniffers. As a rule the sensors of these units will sound an alarm to warn you of danger. You, however, are the best protection your boat can have.

The wise boater is aware of these dangers almost by second nature. what matters most often, are the improvements that you, as a live-aboard, can make to your boat with the intention of making life better while you're living on board. I'll merely point out some items to you, as a potential live aboard, that you may want to be aware of. These are not necessarily in any particular order. If you plan on spending any meaningful time aboard your boat, for whatever reason, you might as well be comfortable.

COOKING STOVES:
Often when new live aboards move onto their boat, the stove that had been used for week-ending, is no longer adequate. You'll want to consider replacing it with something larger. Odds are you don't really need a gimbaled stove. A four-burner stove with a decent oven will be needed to satisfy most female boaters, or anyone who does most of the cooking.

CLOTHES STORAGE
For some career folks, the standard small hanging locker will not be adequate. You can arrange to use an aft quarter berth as a much larger clothes hanging locker by adding a long closet clothes rod. A one and one half inch, or two inch wooden dowel, like the ones used in most home closets will do the job. Suspend it at both ends and it should work out for you. Of course slacks and pants will most likely need to be hung supported in the center, which is folded over the center of the hanger, rather than by the cuffs.

COMPUTERS
This can be a problem for some boaters, but being a writer I always manage to find an area for my system. Generally the main dining table, but this depends on your needs, and the amount of equipment you require. The main problem here is storing your system while underway in rough weather. Out of five computer systems, Lyn and I

have two complete systems, two printers and one large flatbed scanner that have traveled extensively with us. There is always at least one system on the boat. If your mate is not into computers, don't insist on using prime space for your system and in this case a laptop may be the best bet for you.

CUSHIONS
You may want to have many comfortable cushions available. These can fill those recesses behind your back in the corners of your settees. They generally add comfort in many conditions while living aboard.

ELECTRIC HEATER
Small electric heaters are nice to have aboard in the winter months, and it probably won't take a large one to keep you warm. I've always been a bit leery of the fan driven ones, a personal problem, so I use one of those oil filled radiator types. I've virtually left one of these on continually all winter without problems of any kind. Most of the heaters have two or three heat ranges, which works well for the different seasons aboard.

COMPACT DISK PLAYER, TELEVISION, or a RADIO
Nice music is a pleasant thing to have around in most any weather, especially in the winter months.

Of course a television can help in passing the time. You can find television antennas that work quite well, or you can build a simple version for very few dollars yourself. Lyn and I have used a home made antenna for years with quite good results. Okay, I only needed an antenna that would allow her to see her favorite soaps. You don't get cable television with these.

LIGHTING AND OUTLETS:
You can't run everything off the boat's deep cell batteries forever when you move aboard, even if you have an Inverter, for any great length of time. If you don't have shore power, get it. Once you have shore power available, place at least two or three A.C. outlets on each side of the boat, more if possible. These outlets should be wired to at least two breaker switches, four would be better.

Your shore power would be the initial source to this breaker box. Most breaker boxes are placed in an aft locker, generally one that is easily reached from the cockpit. A very useable place on many power boats, would be down inside the aft engine hatch area. Use at least a twelve gauge wire. Keep in mind that the insulation on the outside of the wire cable must be able to stand up to the oil and grease in the harsh environment of your bilge. Most standard wiring is produced with this ability now.

REFRIGERATORS

An ice box is fine for weekends, sometimes even extended cruising. Yet, living aboard in a marina, a small refrigerator is a very nice addition. It need not be a large refrigerator, but it should be big enough to hold a half gallon of milk, perhaps a small package of meat, and other odds and ends.

Generally you can pick one of these up for around a hundred plus dollars. I recommend you get the biggest one you can find space for if you're going to live aboard for an extended period. It will be money well spent. Even after you move back ashore, you will still find a use for the small refrigerator, perhaps in an office or work shop at home.

Cans of soda pop stored in any part of the boat where they come in contact with the outer hull, saves a cooling problem. You will be surprised how cold they will be when kept in this manner. There can be one exception to this idea. If you have any salt water intrusion into your bilge, don't keep aluminum cans down there. Salt water and aluminum cans don't mix well. I once heard of a salt water racing crew who kept cases of beer in their bilge. It wasn't long before the boat smelled like a brewery.

If you are expecting company for a glass of wine, chill it by placing it in a bag, then lower the bag over the side into the cooler water below the boat. I recommend a bag, because I once lost a very good bottle of white wine out of a metal bucket as I was pulling it back up from the cooler depths.

TELEPHONE

This is an easy fix. The telephone company can easily provide you with service to your boat. You may need to contact your marina office for permission, but generally this does not seem to be a problem.

Another solution is, of course, a cellular telephone. You could use your VHF radio as well, but using a credit calling card over the airways can result in someone stealing your numbers off the air. If you choose this method, arrange to call everywhere collect.

BUG SCREENS

During the warmer months you may want to use screens to keep out mosquitos or any offending flying bugs you may not want to feed or entertain with your own body fluids. You can purchase a nylon lingerie fabric called "*Denier*" This is very flexible and can be cut and sewn to fit your needs. Lyn often uses this material for hatch covers with a piece of half inch nylon line sewn into the edge for weight, then she can lay the whole arrangement over the top of an open hatch and easily store it away when not in use.

SOME WATER PROBLEMS

I recommend not using anything on the boat that puts moisture inside the boat. Especially in the winter. On board showers are nice, but unless you have a large water supply, and a method of getting rid of the water overboard immediately, don't use one. The amount of water and moisture they put into your bilge is tremendous. Also the marina may not appreciate the grey water going over the side while you use your shower.

Pressure water systems are also a nice touch but they make you feel the water supply is unlimited. You will be surprised at how much faster you go through your water supply with a pressure system. When you have to pump it manually, it lasts much longer. In the winter months, don't try to make your boat air tight. Let the boat breath. Put up with any small draft by cranking up the heater.

One cure for the shower problem is the use of a garden spray tank. Purchase one new, and get the large three-gallon size. Then remove the spray hose and nozzle, replace it with one of those sink dish sprayer units you would use in your kitchen sink at home . These can be purchased at nearly any hardware store. You pour hot and cold water into the tank, mixed to your liking. Screw the top on and pump it full of air pressure. You will have to pump it occasionally while you shower. When one of these tanks are nearly full, it can actual provide showers, and clean hair, for two people.

In your cockpit you can hang a plastic tarp down from the boom in a sail boat, or from your upper bridge deck on power boats. This allows some privacy, but if used in the chill of winter you won't be out there in the cockpit very long. Lyn and I have used this arrangement for years with good results.

There is one problem about living aboard, I've not shared with you as yet. The problem is this. Once you've lived onboard for any length of time, you will find it difficult to move ashore again. The life style is unique, and living in a home on the beach does not compare.

STORAGE AREAS
Storage space is always a premium problem. No matter the size of the boat, it seems you need one more place for one more item you feel you have to have aboard. As you store things away keep in mind that this can be a hostile environment for some items. One often overlooked storage area is in the center of your vee berth. Yes, that place where you use the step to get up into one berth or the other. Yes, the same step you cover up with a board that just fits, but allows you a full vee berth bed. Once the vee berth filler board is in place, the space under it is mostly wasted space. Yes, the place where you probably have a cardboard box full of stuff. However, you can install a vertical panel across here, and use the inside area for storage. You can even add drawers, or doors to it,

and a shelf. On larger boats, power or sail, a vee berth may not be a problem. Yet there is often potential unused storage area under your raised bedding platform, and more aft in those cockpit lockers.

Sometimes there is an area behind the vertical cushions in your main salon that can be used. On my boat, "Itchy Feet," I used a Sabre saw to cut openings here, like sizable portholes, then used thick foam blocks as locker bottoms. I used foam so as not to restrict any hull flexing. Though I don't believe my hull flexes, I didn't want to restrict any movement in the mid section of the boat. We used this space as long term storage, for paper towels, toilet paper, etc. All paper items require storage in resealable plastic bags for protection. If stored any other way, you may have soggy, wet pulp when you really need dry supplies.

WATER HEATERS
If you check around the various recreational vehicle markets, you can find a small six gallon water heater. These are small enough to fit into, or under some seats, or galley areas. Also, there is a small, one hundred twenty volt water heater that produces hot water on demand for around a hundred dollars. Check with an appliance store, or a water heater supplier for these. They may not work for showers, but for most use they will be very adequate.

IFPublications
mgn.editor@gmail.com

Other books written by Donald Boone

LIVING ABOARD PROJECTS
Moving onboard a boat is when you find there are things that need to be changed to make life aboard better and more comfortable. This book has 43 projects plus other useful information you might find of interest to helping your easement into life aboard, and those who might be joining you.
ISBN 1-882896-02-5
EAN 978-1-882896-02-8

SEXUAL HAPPINESS
Sexual happiness is one of the most important things to happen in your life. This book is designed to help you look for the correct person to have in your life. This kind of search is seldom preformed, but it should be the case in every relationship. Be honest with yourself about your own needs, then use this book to find the best lover to fill your own life.
ISBN 1-882896-16-5
EAN 978-1882896-16-5

Two free natal charts are available if you are the original purchaser of the book, Sexual Happiness or Choosing Lovers.. Contact for details can be made through the e-mail address listed above.

CHOOSING LOVERS
Why spend years with the wrong lover.
Find the one that best suits your needs
and enjoy freedom from sexual hunger.
ISBN 1-882896-04-1
EAN 978-1-882896-04-2

CYCLES & RHYTHMS of INTRIGUE
Most of life, if not all of it, contains cycles.
From the birth of any event it will find
its natural rhythm and follow it to the
end. Is life fated, read the answer in this
book.
ISBN 1-882896-07-6
EAN 978-1-882896-07-3

THE CHESS COACH
Becoming one is easy, and it can be
very rewarding. If you play the game
and have time on your hands, consider
becoming a chess coach.
ISBN 1-882896-08-4
EAN 978-1882896-08-0

THE SEA PILOT
In this age of sailing vessels, we no longer fear sailing
over the edge of the flat world, and we find our way
with compass and chronometer. This was not so when
this story took place.
ISBN 1-882896-09-2
EAN 978-1-882896-09-7

CHESS STORIES THROUGH THE AGES
This book, 'Chess Stories Through The Ages,' contains stories that have been passed from one generation to the next down through history. From why 'White moves first, and an unknown story of 'Helen of Troy, found in, 'The Sacrificed Trojan Horse.'
ISBN 1-882896-10-6
EAN 978-1882896-10-3

THOSE WHO PLAY CHESS
Knowing how your opponent plays chess, his or her favorite pieces and their quirks, are a definite advantage to you in this game. Especially if you play in tournaments. This book will provide you with information on them as individuals, and that of their personalities. You will also find lists of historical players with the same kinds of individualism's and personalities to help guide you in your defense at the table.
ISBN 1-882896-11-4
EAN 978 -1-882896 -11-0

IMPACT
Meteors have been haunting mankind since the beginning of mankind, and they still do. This story is about one of those celestial bodies that does not miss the earth on its path around our sun. Like meteorites of the past, the damage it causes when it strikes the earths surface, is devastating. However, many survive and this story is about how one group came together to get through the worst of the affects.
ISBN 1-882896-12-2
EAN 978-1-882896-12-7

THE CHESS GAME
Having lost a huge sum in prize money due to an oversight in a championship chess game, he became a revenge killer. He spelled it out for his opponents during his killing spree. You will see the connection as you read this story.
ISBN 1-882896-13-0
EAN 978-1882896-13-4

WELCOME ABOARD
When those who have lived around the water, and their day comes to an end, it is time to relax. Whether they are lying in a Vee birth, or on a cushion in the cockpit of a boat. Perhaps even a bed ashore. It doesn't matter as they frequently have an abundance of time. To fill the time they read and let the stories unfold in their mind's as the hours pass by. This book is comprised of stories that take place in this world. A place where you meet life on its terms.
ISBN 1-882896-03-3
EAN 978-1-882896-03-5

www.ingramcontent.com/pod-product-compliance
Lightning Source LLC
Chambersburg PA
CBHW071513040426
42444CB00008B/1623